Costumes for the Stage

Sheila Jackson

Costumes for the Stage

A complete handbook for
every kind of play

Herbert Press

Published by the Herbert Press
an imprint of A & C Black (Publishers) Limited
35 Bedford Row, London WC1R 4JH

First published in Great Britain 1978
by the Herbert Press
Reprinted 1980
Reprinted 1989
First paperback edition 1988
Reprinted 1989, 1992, 1995, 1998

Designed by Gillian Greenwood
Cover design by Pauline Harrison
Printed in Hong Kong by South China Printing Co.

British Library Cataloguing in Publication Data:

Jackson, Sheila
    Costumes for the stage: a complete
    handbook for every kind of play.
    1. Costume
    I. Title
    792'.026   PN2067

ISBN 0-906969-77-8

Contents

Introduction

This book aims at simplicity in all aspects of costume design and making, and involves only processes within the capabilities of the talented amateur or of those already involved in arts and crafts in areas not usually applied to the stage. It is planned so that it can be used with the utmost flexibility and also as a starting point for designers to develop ideas and directions most suited to themselves. I hope that it will encourage an inventive approach to a craft which is an adventure in itself.

The period costumes shown in the drawings are deliberately the simplest versions so that they will be within the scope of the amateur though able person. Occasionally a more elaborate costume is included but is intended only to help set the style of the period. This accounts for what may appear to be omissions, particularly in the tailoring field. If the play requires, for example, nineteenth-century men's evening dress, realistic uniforms or armour, then hiring from a costume rental shop is the most sensible answer to the problem. It will also be considerably cheaper in the long run.

If the performer's own hair can be grown, cut or suitably dressed there will be no problems in this department; otherwise it is best to hire wigs too.

The drawings are also intended to lead to fuller research away from the usual costume books on the local library shelves. Old periodicals and journals with pictorial coverage of places and events (such as *Punch* or *Harper's*) are an excellent source of both fashionable and social reference. Museums are, of course, a major source of information but quite often interesting details appear in unlikely places, such as an eighteenth-century lady on a clock face or some figures at a picnic on the side of an old cup. Medieval sculptures are a particularly good source of head-dress information. Geographical books and magazines have not only regional information but very often historical reference too. Collect museum post-cards, old family photographs and pictures cut from all possible sources and keep them by you and *look* at them. Reference is to be lived with, not tucked away. Three or four cards pinned where you can see them, and changed from time to time, can often be of more use than many hours spent in museums.

It is difficult to recommend the best way for keeping reference material, because every production requires a different cross-section. Clearly labelled boxes are probably the most versatile method.

When the initial design ideas have been discussed with the director and actors, gather your team and resources around you, take stock of your finances, and start planning. A designer needs a back-up team of a number of people with different capabilities – some who are strong on the sewing side and can cut and fit, some who can dye and paint fabrics, and others whose talents lie in trimming and decorating or in using their fingers deftly to make hats, crowns, and jewelry.

The budget will need careful thought. When planning it do not forget the vital though sometimes boring necessities such as shoes, and remember that dyes and sewing materials can become quite a large item.

Last, but by no means least, start work in good time. Staying up all night to get the show on may sound exciting and noble, but mistakes and bad workmanship due to fatigue are the likely result. Bad planning and last minute panic are also expensive, and an early start with plenty of thought will save money, energy and temper.

1 · Planning and equipment

Before starting to design and make costumes for a production it is a good idea to plan your work space so that clean work can be kept separate from dyes, paint and glue and all the equipment you will need is within easy reach.

1 – An area for clean work: designing, cutting out, sewing, fitting and pressing.

Equipment A cutting table with chairs of suitable height; a strong sewing machine capable of sewing all kinds and thicknesses of material; iron and ironing board; an adjustable light; a dress stand, preferably a small size so that it can be padded as necessary (see drawing); a hat block or head block for working on hats, head-dresses and decorative wigs; yardstick, tape measure, pins, needles, scissors, pinking shears; sewing threads, in a tin box or large glass jar for easy selection; marking chalks and a soft pencil; brown paper or newspaper for making patterns; a stock of tapes, bindings, zippers, hooks and eyes, press studs, buttons, etc. in marked boxes; cardboard boxes – large, to hold dress fabrics, and smaller to hold trimmings.

2 – An area for messy work – painting, gluing, dyeing, cutting and sawing, hammering, etc. A strong, rigid table is essential, and it is useful to have a sink with running water and a gas burner or electric ring within easy reach.

Equipment A zinc bath or bucket for dyeing; a kettle and an old saucepan; scissors, pliers, hack saw, coarse cheese grater (for breaking down fabrics), Stanley (matt) knife and blades, hand drill, eyelet punch, ruler; jars, plastic pots and all kinds of container; paint and glue brushes; plastic bags, various sizes; quantities of newspaper; a small stapling machine; some kind of protective screen for use when spraying paint, etc. On a convenient shelf, in carefully labelled bottles or boxes, keep white spirit (turps substitute), methylated spirit (denatured alcohol), shellac, dyes; gummed paper tape; adhesives; cold water paste; galvanized wire and fuse wire; carpet thread and needles.

Do not throw away plastic containers of any shape or size, old sponges, egg boxes, corrugated cardboard, cardboard tubes, rope and string of various kinds, odd pieces of timber and hardboard (masonite), beads, buttons, buckles and belts, corks, bottle caps, cotton reels. Train yourself to recognize the potentialities of all kind of waste material.

Collect the nucleus of a basic wardrobe Use old trunks, hampers, suitcases or large boxes and tea chests to store cast-off leotards, sweaters, blouses and shirts, pyjama trousers, simple swimming costumes and trunks, bikinis, tights and socks, felt and straw hats. Boots, shoes and other footwear should be kept in a separate box. Collect cast-off fur and fur-fabric coats for trimmings; old sheets, blankets, tablecloths, curtains, bedspreads etc. for cutting into. Store in plastic sacks any old clothes which will come in useful for character costumes or for breaking down into rags. Save old spectacle frames and junk jewelry. If there is space for a hanging rail or rod, this can be used to store costumes from previous productions; an old sheet thrown over it will keep the garments reasonably clean.

Buying new material Sensible and economic shopping mainly depends on being quite clear about the goods you need and the purpose to which they will be put. Get to know the shops in your neighbourhood and their particular specialities. Train yourself to have a good eye for the possibilities of unusual objects and materials, and to have the foresight to pick up bargains for future use. Market stalls are not as cheap as they used to be but can still be useful, and cut-price fabric shops can sometimes be found in market areas.

If you have collected a store of fabrics, keep a loose-leaf book with clippings from these stapled to pages noting the yardage, so that it is clear at a glance what is in stock.

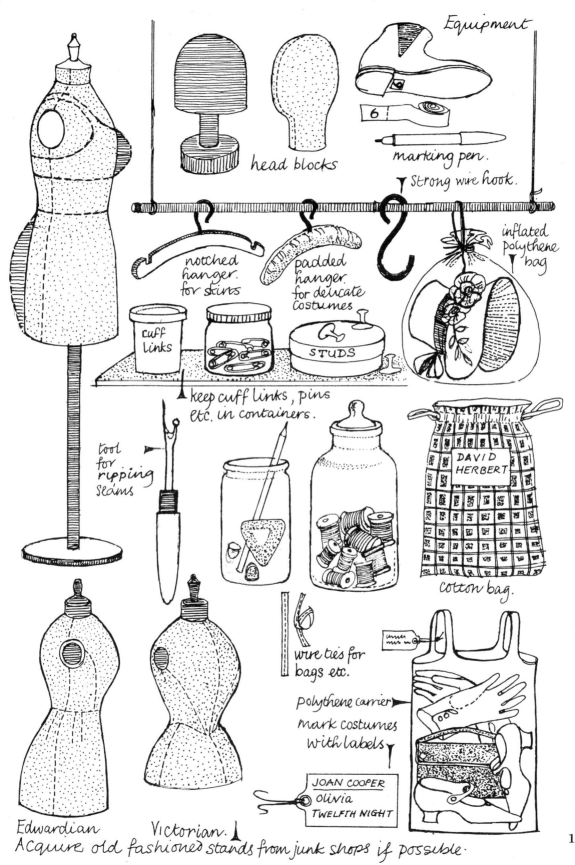

Equipment

head blocks

marking pen.

Strong wire hook.

notched hanger. for skirts

padded hanger. for delicate costumes

inflated polythene bag

cuff links

STUDS

keep cuff links, pins etc. in containers.

tool for ripping seams

DAVID HERBERT

cotton bag.

wire ties for bags etc.

polythene carrier

mark costumes with labels

JOAN COOPER
Olivia
TWELFTH NIGHT

Edwardian   Victorian.

Acquire old fashioned stands from junk shops if possible.

2 · Measurements, patterns and fitting

Keep a book or card index containing the measurements of all the people taking part in a production. The most important measurements are:

Women – height, bust, waist, hips, nape to waist, waist to ground, across back, outer-arm bent, shoulder seam, wrist, and neck; the measurement from shoulder over bust point to waist can also be helpful.

Men – height, chest, waist, inside leg, nape to waist, across back, outer-arm bent, shoulder seam, jacket length, collar size; and, for robes, waist to ground.

It is easier for two people to take measurements, one using the tape measure, the other writing the measurements down. Make sure the subject is standing upright, and do not pull the tape too tightly. When measuring a large and sensitive person it is tactful not to shout out the measurements in front of other people. Remember to ask for the shoe size, a lot of people are dishonest about this. Instep and calf measurements are essential for boots, which can be difficult for people with a high instep.

For hats and wigs three basic measurements are needed: head circumference, distance from ear to ear over the head, and distance from forehead to the base of the skull.

The patterns in this book on squared paper are drawn to a scale of $\frac{1}{4}$in to 2in (i.e. each square represents 2in) and are based on a person of average size. The basic shape can often be adapted to a variety of garments by altering the neckline, the shape of the sleeves, the length etc. (Note abbreviations: c.b. – centre back; c.f. – centre front; D.B. – double-breasted.) The diagrammatic patterns included in some of the drawings are not to scale, being only a guide to shape. It is not possible to give the quantity of fabric required as fabrics come in a variety of widths. The layout of pattern pieces is also governed by the width of the fabric. A little experimentation with the pieces will show the most economical arrangement.

Draft the pattern on strong brown paper or newspaper, measuring outwards from centre front and centre back and adapting the measurements to fit the actor. Lay out the fabric on a large table and pin the pattern in position, with centre back and front on a fold where indicated, allowing about an inch all round for seams and turnings. Cut with large, sharp scissors and mark the darts and openings with tailor's chalk. Keep all patterns in large clearly-labelled envelopes for future use; make a sketch on the outside for easy identification and add the height and bust or chest size.

It is much easier to fit a garment if it has been stitched rather than tacked (basted) – use a large stitch so that it can easily be unpicked; a seam

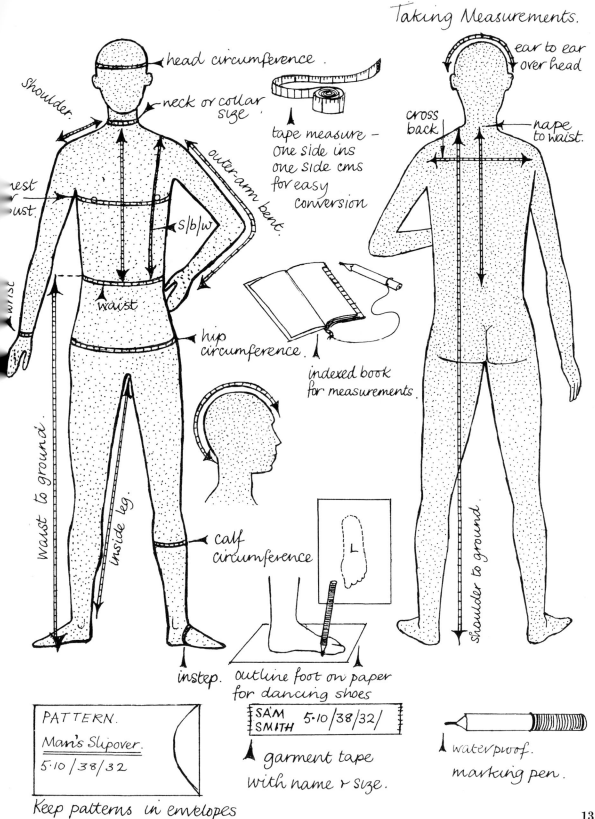

Taking Measurements.

head circumference.

neck or collar size

Shoulder.

outer-arm bent.

s/b/w

chest
bust

wrist

waist

waist to ground.

inside leg.

hip circumference.

calf circumference

instep.

ear to ear over head

cross back

nape to waist.

shoulder to ground.

tape measure – one side ins one side cms for easy conversion

indexed book for measurements

outline foot on paper for dancing shoes

L

PATTERN.

Man's Slipover.

5·10 / 38 / 32

Keep patterns in envelopes

SAM SMITH   5·10 / 38 / 32 /

garment tape with name & size.

waterproof. marking pen.

ripper is available for unpicking stitches (see drawing) and is invaluable for fast work. Leave sensible seam allowances – too little makes adjustment impossible, too much makes for clumsy fitting. Fitting should always de done with the garment inside out. Adjustments are usually best made on the shoulder seams and side seams – be sure to keep the grain of the fabric true, otherwise the garment will not hang properly. A waist seam makes it easier to adapt a garment to a high or low waist. Always leave a good hem so that the costume can be worn by a taller person at a later date. Mark the garment with a name tape, and also with the size so that it can be fitted to another actor if necessary.

Fat characters Actors taking the part of fat people, from the slightly plump to the Falstaffian, will have to be helped with padding when their own physique is inadequate. If a woman needs only a small increase in size a little padding can be slipped inside a stretch bra or panty-girdle and held in place with a few stitches – (Dacron or Terylene wadding is the best kind as it is light, uncrushable and washable). For sagging breasts use soft cloth bags filled with birdseed fastened into a large-sized bra – these have very realistic movement! Large paddings for women and all paddings for men must be built up on a leotard in the same way as for the peascod doublet on page 41. Build the shape up gradually, layer by layer, stitching in place as you go. It is difficult to make fat arms and legs convincingly; whenever possible cover them with sleeves, trousers and boots. Remember that a thin neck and face cannot be altered and can look ridiculous with an enormous body.

It goes without saying that the padding must be completed before the garment which is to go over it can be cut and fitted.

3 · The changing shape of period costume

Two important considerations when designing costumes are shape and colour. Whereas it is possible to eliminate the colour aspect by designing in black, white and grey – as in the early days of television – it is impossible to create a costume which has no shape. Costumes with bad or weak shapes are all too common and it is necessary to train the eye to select what is telling and pertinent and to incorporate these elements into the design. This chapter sketches the changing shape of period clothes; but it should not be thought that the consideration of shape applies only to historical dress – it is just as important when designing a comedy horse or a spaceman's costume, neither of which are in any way related to the historical scene.

The drawings show women and men from the early medieval period to the 1930's. I have tried to select figures which will show fairly clearly the progression of costume style. Transitional styles – often very interesting – have necessarily had to be left out. Change of shape is affected by the social history of the period, the availability and discovery of fabrics, the human desire for change which creates fashion, and the convenience of certain shapes of garment according to the wearer's way of life. In early days fashion, and therefore shape, changed very slowly; this has accelerated until today fashion changes almost yearly.

Women Early medieval dress is simple, falling easily to the ground from the small bust and over the full hips. Early paintings of Adam and Eve show the fashionable woman's body of the period – tiny breasts, large belly and thin stick-like arms; medieval dress should emphasize this. Shoes are flat, and a plain wimple (head cloth) completely hides the hair. The gradual change to the high medieval period continues to stress the small bust, the dress is still cut without a waist seam, emphasizing the high waist with fullness pulled into pleats by a belt. The sleeves have widened to a bell shape. Note the elaboration of the wimple worn over horns.

The Tudor woman becomes more square. The bodice is stiff, the waist only slightly higher than normal, the bell-shaped sleeves are turned back to form heavy cuffs. The overdress may be split down the front, the square neck emphasizes solidity. The Elizabethan woman is exaggerated and padded, with a stiff and by now very long bodice, a small waist stressed by the cartwheel skirt, and the face framed by an elaborate collar or ruff instead of a wimple. Following this stiffness comes the softer, more rounded shape of Charles I's reign. The ruff has become a soft collar, the skirt has also collapsed from its stiff shape, tabs replace the pleated peplum and the waist has risen. This softness continues during the Restoration period although the waist is again lower.

The artificial quality of the eighteenth century leads to more exaggeration – a long corseted bodice and side-panniered skirt which, in high fashion, extends sideways in an almost unwieldly manner. In many dresses there is an Arcadian effect; ladies at this time liked to imagine themselves in the role of shepherdesses. By the second half of the century the side fullness has been gathered to the back and the previously small muslin cap has grown to an immense size to accommodate the high powdered wig. By the turn of the century the waistline is immediately under the breasts and the silhouette is long and narrow, reminiscent of ancient Greece. Flimsy fabrics imported from India become popular.

Primness, the hallmark of Victoria's long reign, is reflected in the bell-shaped skirt of 1840 with tight corseted bodice and minute waist. By the 1880's prettiness has given way to a poker uprightness and rigidity, with the skirt supported by a bustle at the back. Edwardian waists continue small, but the gored skirt facilitates movement; sleeves have swelled out to the leg-of-mutton shape, hats are getting bigger. By 1910 both hat and coiffure are huge, the fashion now is for the mature figure and the skirt is very narrow around the ankles, giving a top-heavy silhouette.

The 1914–18 war brought emancipation for women, reflected in their dress; by the 1920's the restrictions of corsets have gone, low waists and straight lines flatter the boyish figure, and suddenly legs are on view! A more feminine softness creeps in during the thirties, but with no loss of mobility.

Men The early medieval man wears a simple magyar tunic and a hood; loose trousers are tied round his legs with thongs. As the period progresses this basic shape is elaborated to become theatrical and dandyish. Gradually the very pointed outline becomes more square, giving way by the early sixteenth century to the shape familiarized by portraits of Henry VIII and playing card figures. Elaboration continues – the Elizabethan man, like his female counterpart, is slashed and padded with a long peascod doublet and puffed shoulders and breeches. His face is also framed by an elaborate ruff or collar. By the time of Charles I slashing is still fashionable and the softer silhouette is trimmed with ribbons. Further extravagances lead, in mid-seventeenth century, to a heavily lace-trimmed, be-ribboned, comic figure with huge periwig and enormous boots.

The stylish eighteenth-century man introduces the arrival of the frock coat, full-skirted and deeply cuffed. The hair is neatly held back in a pigtail and capped by a smart tricorne, fine lace shows at the neck and wrists. Later a narrower shape develops; the coat has lost its fan pleats at the side and, by the turn of the century, the front skirts are cut away and the coat sports a collar.

The frock coat of the 1840's is severe, and men's clothes now begin to take on a sober aspect. Trousers become usual, as does the top hat. By the end of the nineteenth century the familiar suit begins to emerge, becoming more casual as different forms of jacket are developed – smoking jackets, blazers, etc., more appropriate to the informal activities of twentieth-century living.

(13 — plain wimple

tight sleeves

simple robe ►

note high waist — (15)

The Changing Shape

gable head-dress

simple hood and tunic

cocks comb type hat called chaperon

Flamboyant (15)

The square shape like. Playing cards 1535

shirt frill

tight sleeves. (13)

very pointed shoes called poulaines

bun toed shoes

17

High Elizabethan. stiff shape

Charles I

rounded shape.

Charles II

The puffed & padded figure

Elizabethan Man.

note peascod doublet

Charles I approx 1635

1666

petticoat breeches

First half of the C18

little mob cap becomes big mob cap

2nd half of the C18

straw hat

Empire Note high waist & emphasis on vertical lines

First half of C18

large cuff

fiddle-skirt

2nd half of C18

no cuff

narrow skirt

1806

19

1840

The rounded shape, all lines lead to the waist

1880's

1895

leg of mutton sleeves.

note bottleneck shape of both men + women

1840

double breasted reefer

1888

Late C19

1910

Straight lines — girlish figure.

— low. Waist

1926 Skirts reach their shortest.

softer and more flowing lines

natural waist

1933. Longer skirts

n.b high waistline

Smoking jacket with dress trousers 1912

1920's

knitted Cardigan

plus fours

1930's

21

4 · Greek drama

Costumes for Greek plays are easy to make and can be made on a fairly low budget from butter muslin (cheesecloth), old sheets, towelling (terrycloth) and old curtains. If you can afford them, soft crêpe (particularly wool crêpe) and various kinds of jersey will give more sophisticated results as they drape especially well, and artificial silk jersey is excellent for an elegant woman's dress. But cheaper fabrics can give interesting and rewarding results and can often be enriched with painted pattern and texture. Extra depth and texture can also be added by spraying the garment here and there with paint or dye after it is made up (see page 106); this should be done on a dress stand so that the three-dimensional effect can be seen. Do not spray too thickly or the drapery will look stiff.

The clothes of ancient Greece are very simple in shape, so to avoid monotony the overall design of a production must be particularly well thought out. The chorus plays a vital part in Greek plays and should be seen as a mass rather than as a number of individual people. It is a good idea to have the same basic costume for all the actors with small differences in pattern or colour within the group; too much variation spoils the grandeur of the massed performance. Remember that the chorus binds the play together verbally and should therefore achieve the same effect visually. Stylized wigs, head-dresses or even masks can help to overcome the actors' physical differences, and the impersonal quality of either full or half masks can be very successful here; if a great deal of speaking is involved, they will be more comfortable made from latex (see page 110), but the main consideration should be lightness of weight.

The principal actors play against this background, and the emphasis of their costumes should be heightened with colour and detail to add visual impact to the drama.

There are three basic garments – the cloak or *chlamys*, a rectangular piece of material about twice as long as its width, which can be worn in various ways; the tunic or *chiton*, worn by both men and women, which can be long or short, simple or pleated; and the overdress or *peplos*, an overgarment worn only by women which is often folded over at the top (see pattern, page 28) and may be girded with rope, cord or braid either over or under the fold.

The drawings on pages 23 and 25 are taken from ancient Greek pottery, and can easily be adapted for the stage. The first (*a*) shows a cloak over a simple tunic. In *b* a much larger cloak is worn over a tunic, both heavily patterned – the cloak could be stencilled whereas the tunic needs free brush work (see chapter 16). In *c* a servant girl wears an under-tunic, an over-tunic and a cloak; in *d* the tunic is bloused over a girdle. A young boy (*e*) wears a short tunic with a leopard skin slung across it; an imitation skin

Ancient greece

This pattern could be stencilled

make crosses with felt pen

(a)

(b)

(c)

(d)

hole for thong

shoulder strap

hole + thong

hole for thong

sleeve opening

cf

(e)

(f)

pattern suitable for drawing with felt pen.

(g)

23

could be used, painted canvas would be decorative, or knotted tufts of rug wool could be stitched or glued to provide texture. Make small eyelet holes as shown in the diagram and use a leather thong to tie the skin in place. (Eyelets and thongs or ties are an excellent way of securing some costumes – a simple method which also looks authentic.) The flautist (*f*) wears a short shirt over a long tunic, and the woman (*g*) also wears a short shirt, and a rectangle of cloth wound round the lower part of her body to form a skirt. Examples of both border and spot patterns are shown – the red ground vases are a rich source of such patterns.

The costumes of the later Greek period are more dependent on drapery than on pattern, although border designs are still frequently seen. The young man (*h*) wears a tunic bloused over a girdle and girded above this, with a small cloak clasped at the neck. The woman's pleated dress (*i*) has clasps along the tops of the arms to form sleeves and is worn with a lightweight cloak elaborately draped; *j* shows another pleated dress with cloak, and *k* shows a large cloak very handsomely worn.

To make a tunic with random pleating, use butter muslin (cheesecloth) or very thin cotton fabric, allowing three times the pattern width. Stitch the side seams, then thoroughly soak the fabric before starting to pleat it. Two people are needed to hold the fabric tightly stretched lengthwise while it is folded into one-inch pleats and then tied at intervals with tapes to hold the pleats firmly without digging into the material. Make sure it is absolutely dry before removing the ties.

Footwear presents little difficulty – flat-heeled sandals and espadrilles can easily be adapted. Other ideas are included on the page of details. Note particularly the two wigs on this page; for these make tight-fitting caps of net or thin felt and build on to them with felt shapes which can be stiffened with shellac to give a sculptural look. Beards can be built up in the same way. The heads for the animal skins can be made like masks in latex or papier mâché (page 110) and stitched to the skins, or made from buckram and covered with cloth or felt. Easier still would be to make the skin of painted canvas complete with the head, in this case disregarding the three-dimensional aspect.

The patterns on pages 27 and 28 can be adapted by extending the width according to the sleeve length required and by altering the length to reach knee, calf or ankle, allowing for over-folds or looping up. Catch the edges together at the shoulders and along the arms with decorative clasps made from large buttons, various types of metal or plastic container tops, ties of leather or braid, or shells glued to a felt or leather base and stitched into position. (See also chapter 17.)

Ancient Greece

pattern suitable for stencilling.

h

clasps hold drapery on arm

i

j

Helmet of Athene

k

rectangle of cloth held on left shoulder.

border pattern – could be drawn with a felt pen

25

open toed sandals

2 shoes from a greek vase

adapt socks

Thonged sandal. Use rope soles or soles cut from industrial felt to which loops of tape are stitched to take thonging.

Garland - cut leaves of felt net or leather, **glue** wire veins in place + bind with fuse wire to cord.

elastic ankle support

paint when stretched on foot. Felt shape stitch in place on anklet.

4 sectioned felt cap makes base for wigs.

Plastic dustbin lids make base for shields

velcro fastening

greaves

leather ties

26

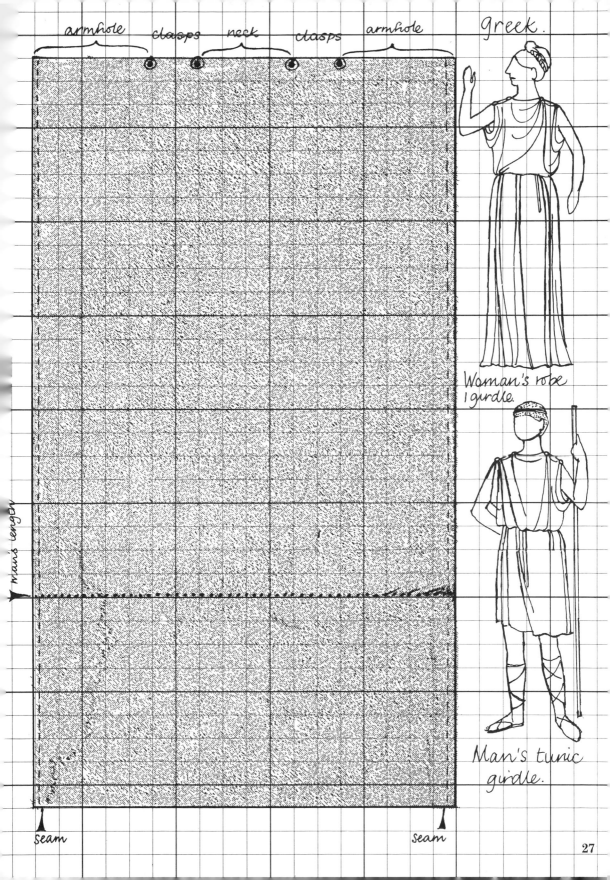

armhole · clasps · neck · clasps · armhole

Greek.

man's length

seam · seam

Woman's robe
& girdle.

Man's tunic
& girdle.

27

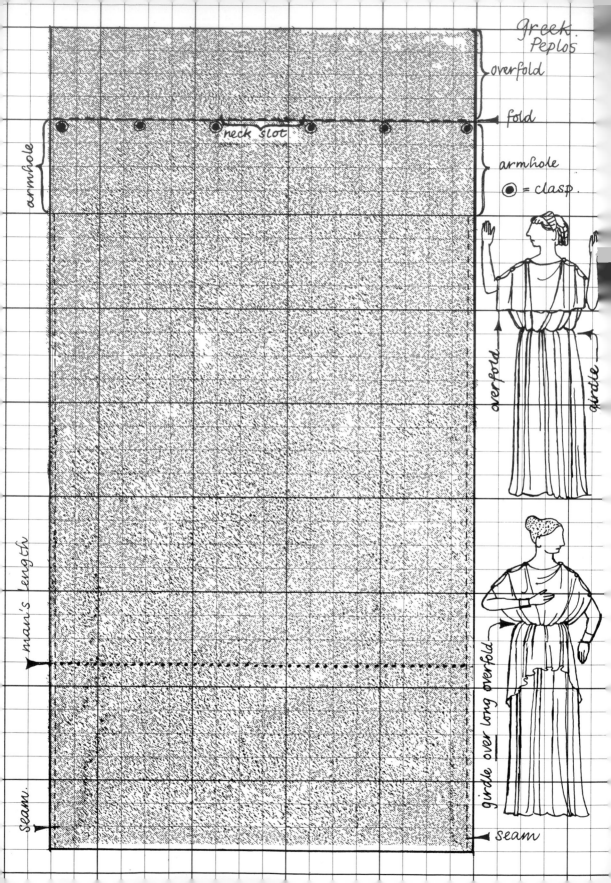

greek.
Peplos

overfold

fold

neck slot

armhole

◉ = clasp.

armhole

man's length

seam.

overfold

girdle

girdle over long overfold

seam

5 · Medieval costume, miracles and mysteries

Medieval costume is very suitable for the miracle plays of the Middle Ages and can also be used for nativity plays and for some Shakespeare productions. Early missals and psalters are full of delightful illustrations drawn with humour and great detail and are well worth studying for ideas. Note their simplicity of statement, and make drawings from them so that you become familiar with the shape of the costumes and with the details so lovingly recorded which will add character to your production.

The drawings here show a variety of garments which could easily be translated into theatrical terms. The basic shape of clothes changes very little throughout the Middle Ages. They are easy to make, and the patterns given on pages 35–7 can be adapted to suit almost any character. There are many ways of arranging the fullness into folds, twisting, knotting and girding the garments, and wearing them belted or loose. It is better to arrange the drapery each time the garment is worn, as permanently fixed drapery tends to become very limp and flat and can also present ironing problems. The best materials to use are those which drape easily such as brushed rayon, soft wools and bolton sheeting (twill cotton). Old sheets and blankets can be used successfully, dyed and sprayed to suit your design. For men's clothes, felt and hessian (burlap) are good for a number of purposes; sacking and towelling (terrycloth) sprayed and painted are helpful in creating rough and heavy textures for peasant characters and primitive effects.

Pattern 1 is the dalmatica, a simple early garment suitable for use in biblical and miracle plays. It is laid out with the centre back and front on the fold of double fabric. The amount of swing in the skirt can be varied: z is the point from which the arc of the skirt is swung and should coincide with the hip bone. Piece x completes the sleeve length, and y is the extra piece which will be needed for a very full skirt. Often a band of pattern is found round the edge of the skirt (some ideas for patterns are on pages 32 and 34).

Pattern 2 is a tunic, another very basic garment useful for many medieval characters. It can be cut with long or short sleeves and a variety of necklines; open at the front, it becomes a rough coat. This pattern can also be used for peasants of any period and many countries. Make it in coarse hessian (burlap), felt, leather, canvas or heavy wool.

Pattern 3 is a robe with magyar sleeves adaptable for male or female wear. Painted or decorated, it is excellent for kings, merchants and rich characters, but it can be used plain for monks, nuns and simple people. It is similar in shape to the robe worn in many Arab countries today. It can be made in various lengths, and the sleeve length or shape can also be altered to suit the character. To obtain pleasing folds, use a fabric which is not too stiff.

The patterns for the hoods on page 37 show various shapes and adaptations. Use fairly soft fabrics such as cotton jersey, wool or thin felt.

Male headgear is commonly the hood, sometimes attached to a cloak (opposite, *f* and *g*), the bag hat (*a*) or the chaperon, a length of scalloped felt or a stiffened fabric fixed to a padded roll and arranged coxcomb fashion (*b*). Other details show a neck-hugging collar (*c*) made from felt, a traveller's hat (*d*), a peasant (*e*), a shepherd with a felt hat and drinking cup (*f*), and a warmly-clad traveller (*h*). Thick socks with rolled tops worn over sneakers are an easy solution for many of the shoes shown in the illustrations, and look convincing. The young man (*j*) wears the short doublet, long hose and pointed shoes typical of the fifteenth century.

Except for the occasional use of the hood by some peasant women, the wimple is the universal form of female headgear. Its main purpose was to hide the hair and make a pleasing frame for the face. The wimple is usually made of two lengths of cloth, one drawn firmly under the chin and fixed with a pin on top of the head, the second laid across the top of the head so that it can be drawn tightly across the forehead and fixed to the first piece at the temples using straight pins. Soft cotton cloth such as a well-worn sheet will look well. Page 34 (*a*) shows the most common form of wimple; *b* is a wimple with a chinstrap of fabric on the double; *c* has a larger drape under the chin and a half circle over the top of the head, the straight edge across the forehead. A full circle could also be used, held in place by a simple circlet. For a grander form of wimple the veil is draped over a flowerpot shape made from buckram – glue the sides of piece *x* together, glue the tabs of the crown *y*, and assemble, *z*. Another style (*d*) shows a hood and black silk veil worn over two small buckram horns fixed to a cloth base tied to the head with tapes.

Some costumes especially for miracle or nativity plays are shown on page 38. The bishop's mitre (*a*) can be cut from felt, canvas or even card and fixed to a skull cap of cloth or felt. The Virgin (*b*) wears a crown (see page 110) over a head veil. Angels can easily become sentimentalized, but many medieval angels are very strong in design and the one shown here from Ethiopia would look very splendid painted in rich golds, oranges and reds. The devil's mask (*d*) can be based on a felt hood, or a latex mask obtainable from a carnival shop could be adapted; striped stockings, painted jersey trousers, and a slightly padded leotard painted with a fearsome design complete the costume. The diagrams for making the tail (*e*) can also be followed for constructing tails for other beasts and birds. Make a pair of trunks or a jock strap; the elastic for the part round the waist must be very strong and grip tightly. Cut a disc of strong leather. Cut tail feathers from felt and stitch or glue to them wire ribs which protrude 8in from the base. Bind these ribs to a 3-in section if broomstick, bending the ends into loops which are then stitched firmly to the leather disc. Then stitch the disc to the back of the trunks. For the eastern king's giant turban head-dress (*f*), use the balloon method described on page 134, and make a beard from felt strips or coarse string stitched to a net base.

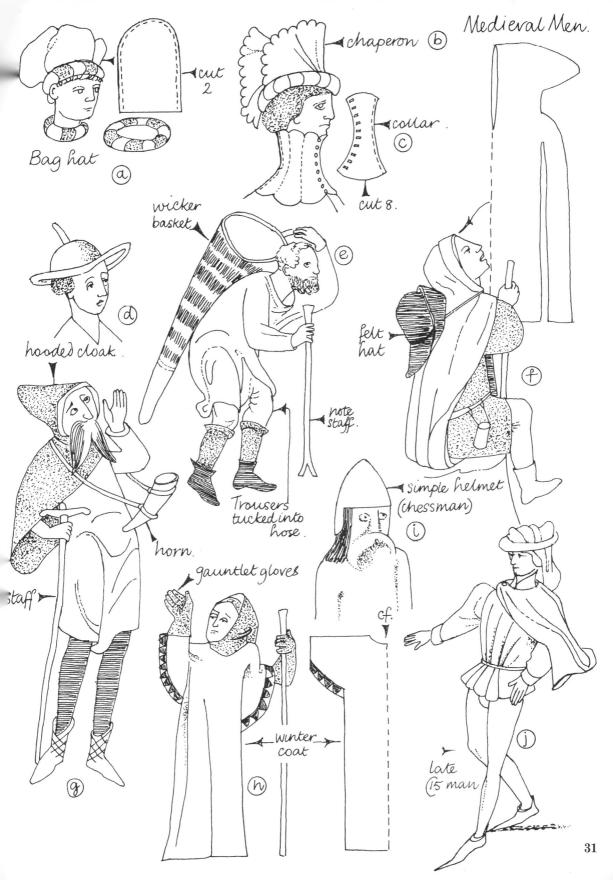

Medieval Men.

Bag hat ⓐ

cut 2

chaperon ⓑ

collar ⓒ

cut 8.

wicker basket

note staff.

ⓔ

felt hat

ⓕ

hooded cloak. ⓓ

horn.

staff

Trousers tucked into hose.

simple helmet (chessman) ⓘ

ⓖ

gauntlet gloves

winter coat

cf.

late 15 man

ⓗ

ⓙ

straw hat.

linen cap.

Tunic tucked up round waist & tied with cord

A traveller with his cloak & bundle carried on a stick.

Basic armour shape cut in jersey & glue or stitch foil or cardboard discs to represent metal plates. Spray silver.

Musician with parti-coloured tunic.

Shepherd in skin tunic, rags tied round legs & feet.

tunic tucked in girdle.

32

this pattern should be drawn with a broad felt pen.

rough linen working apron.

linen strip

Medieval. Women

sleeve less overdress.

wimple worn over horns

net holding hair

Woman holding up skirt to show short hose

make hanging sleeve trimmings from felt.

looped belt.

grand C15 Lady.

dress with hanging oversleeves.

Lady in the stocks showing footwear.

Medieval Details

ⓐ

ⓑ

ⓒ

ⓓ

ⓨ

2×a

b ⓑ

ⓒ

ⓧ

ⓒ

ⓩ

Wimples

ⓓ

ⓓ

sleeveless over-dress or cotehardie

ⓓ

cloth wound round padded roll

cambric hood

knotted head-cloth

a mesh hairnet

A miserly woman showing ragged dress, & apron & big money bag.

skirt of over-dress tucked up

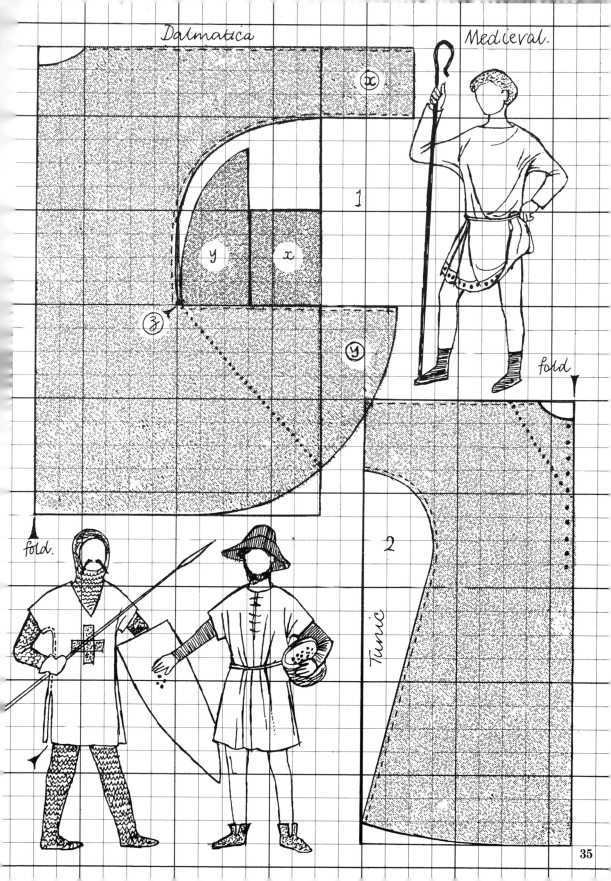

Dalmatica

Medieval.

x

1

y x

3

y

fold

fold.

Tunic

2

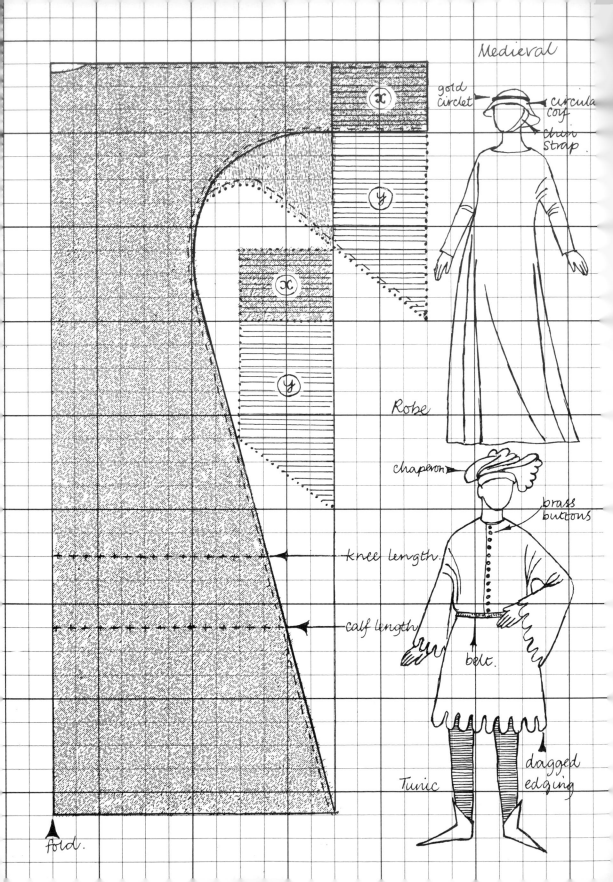

Medieval

gold circlet

circular coif

chin strap

Robe

chaperon

brass buttons

knee length.

calf length

belt.

Tunic

dagged edging

fold.

ⓧ

ⓨ

ⓧ

ⓨ

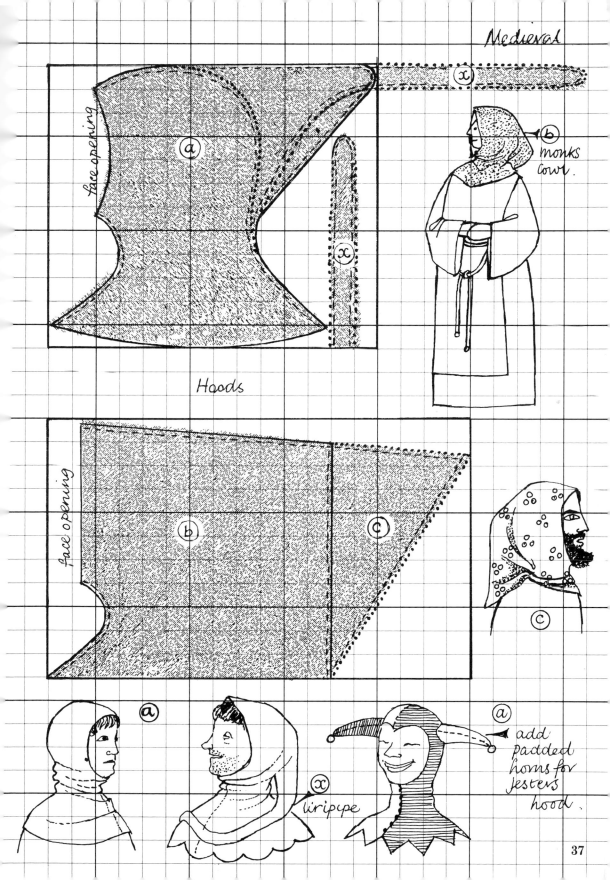

face opening

ⓐ

ⓧ

ⓧ

ⓑ monks cowl.

Hoods

face opening

ⓑ

ⓒ

ⓒ

ⓐ

ⓧ liripipe

ⓐ add padded horns for jesters hood.

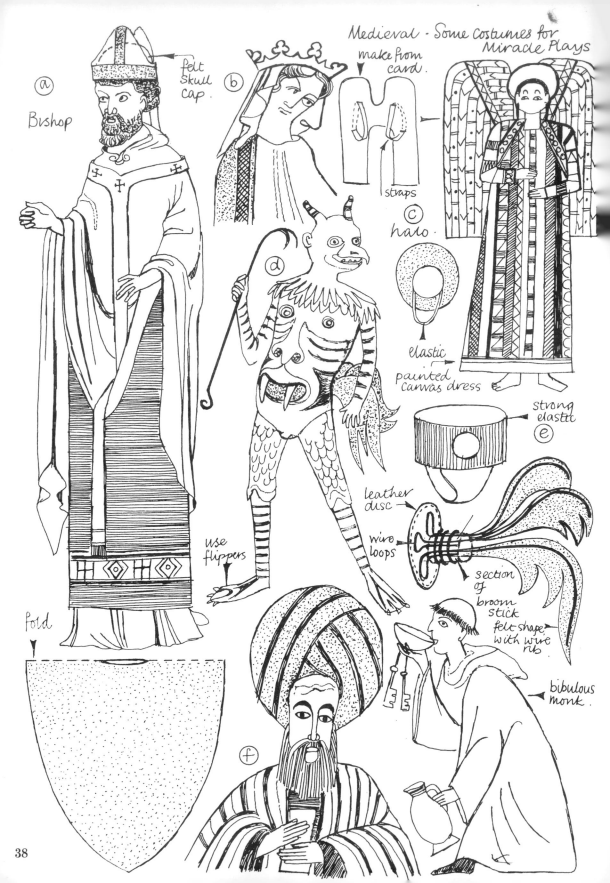

Medieval · Some Costumes for Miracle Plays

ⓐ Bishop

felt skull cap.

ⓑ make from card.

straps

ⓒ halo

ⓓ

elastic

painted canvas dress

ⓔ strong elastic

leather disc

wire loops

section of broom stick

felt shape with wire rib

use flippers

fold

ⓕ

bibulous monk.

6 · Shakespeare and the sixteenth century

The popularity and educational aspect of Shakespeare's plays leads to their frequent performance in schools and colleges. There is no need, of course, for them to be played in the costume of Shakespeare's time – they are often transposed to different periods and this can bring out fresh significance – but if Elizabethan costume is chosen for a production the great elaboration of dress at this time can present a number of problems. The sixteenth century was an age rich in pattern and decoration when wealthy people were very sumptuously dressed. Among poorer and country people the change from the medieval period was slow, and simple tunics, dresses and headgear were still common. For tradesmen and townspeople a simplified version of the fashionable silhouette can be carried out in cheaper and more serviceable fabrics.

The stiffly puffed and padded shape of sixteenth-century costume can be built up as illustrated on page 41. For the man's puffed breeches, use a well-fitting pair of bathing trunks and build on to these with layers of padding or thin sheets of foam rubber. To do this successfully the trunks must be in a stretched state, either on the wearer or on a dress stand; in the latter case first unpick the crutch seam. When a satisfactory shape has been achieved, cover the padding with a layer of cheap cotton jersey which can be sprayed or painted, decorated and braided as desired. Panes, or strips of fabric, can be stitched over the basic shape. For the longer breeches, adapt the pattern on page 50. Build up the shape of the peascod doublet in the same way, layer by layer, onto either a leotard or a tightly fitting sweater which can be held taut with an elasticated jock strap between the legs.

The support for the woman's skirt can be a pair of kidney-shaped hip pads (x), a hip roll (y) or a hoop called a farthingale (z) (page 41). The size of these depends on the style and character of the dress, from the insignificant to the grotesque. Hip pads and rolls are easy to make, as shown. The farthingale is a little more complicated: for simplicity, use a child's hoop, either plastic or wooden, or some very stout cane soaked until pliable and then bound into a circle; it needs to be rigid. This is held in place by a circle of cotton fabric. Use the hoop to draw a pattern. The length of material required equals the circumference of the hoop plus seam allowance, the width is the distance a–b plus seam allowance. Lay out the fabric and draw and cut out four gores as shown in the diagram. Join the seams, leaving a placket opening. Gather the tops of the gores and stitch to a waistband. Stitch facing to the outer edge of the circle, place hoop in position and then stitch the inner edge of the facing over it. A weight or small bag of lead shot fixed to the front of the hoop will cause the farthingale to tilt slightly forward which gives the skirt the correct shape. When making a skirt to wear over the farthingale, remember to allow extra length to cover the width of the hoop (see skirt shapes, page 132).

Some ideas for making ruffs are included in the diagrams on the same page. Use either milliner's nylon crin (available in different widths) or nylon net, as these can easily be rinsed out by shaking in warm water and detergent – an important consideration. Catch the edges with thread at equidistant intervals. If a decorative edging is required, such as gold braid or lace, this should be machined into place along the edge before making up the ruff. Attach the inner side of the ruff to a cambric neckband and fasten with small hooks and eyes and press studs as shown.

To make bun-toed shoes, pad the fronts of elasticated plimsolls, or adapt soft bedroom slippers by adding leather remnants or felt shapes and trimming them with ribbon bows and rosettes.

The two pages of research drawings in this section give shapes and ideas for costumes and also details which may be stylized or adapted for simple presentation. As Elizabethan dress is so complicated some compromise will most likely have to be made, so having achieved as good a period silhouette as possible complement this with well-chosen but simple details and accessories, either painted or applied in a stylized way.

Page 44 offers some suggestions for stylization added to the basic shapes already discussed. The drawings show epaulettes, either stiffened or padded; and the use of braid, ribbons, buttons, painted stripes and stencilled designs. Slashing, which is typical of the period, can be represented by cutout fabric shapes glued into place with Copydex (Sobo in the US).

The addition of a stiffened stomacher (use stiff felt or several layers of vilene or staflex interfacing) helps the appearance of the woman's dress. This can be painted, stencilled, appliquéd or even embroidered.

Semi-circular cloaks can be dramatically used in various lengths.

Tights are an essential part of the Elizabethan man's wardrobe; thin-legged actors can wear several thick pairs on top of one another to help the appearance of their legs. Thick nylon tights are easily dyed and all tights can be painted but this must be done on a pair of display legs. The upper part of the tights can be painted to simulate canions, the thigh-fitting extensions to puffed breeches shown on page 44.

The fabrics worn by rich Elizabethans were very sumptuous indeed – brocades, velvets and rich silks were the order of the day; but a production dressed basically in stout cottons and canvas lavishly painted and sprayed in glowing bronzes and golds could be very effective, as could a production restricted to dramatic black, white, gold and just one colour. Working on these lines can solve many problems and achieve a most successful result.

farthingale

hip pads

ⓧ

cut 4. Stitch & fill with foam or kapok.

tapes for tying

hip roll.

ⓨ

cut 2

Stitch & fill

a

b

c

child's hoop

gather

a

a

c

b

cut 4

ⓩ

hip roll

peascod front. padded area

farthingale

Weight.

c.b opening

stitch

stitch

pearl beads

stitch

stitch

construction of ruff.

Build padding on to swimming trunks

sneakers with elasticated inset

Bun toed shoe

pad toe on outside with wadding & cover with jersey fabric

cambric neck band.

poppers. (large snaps)

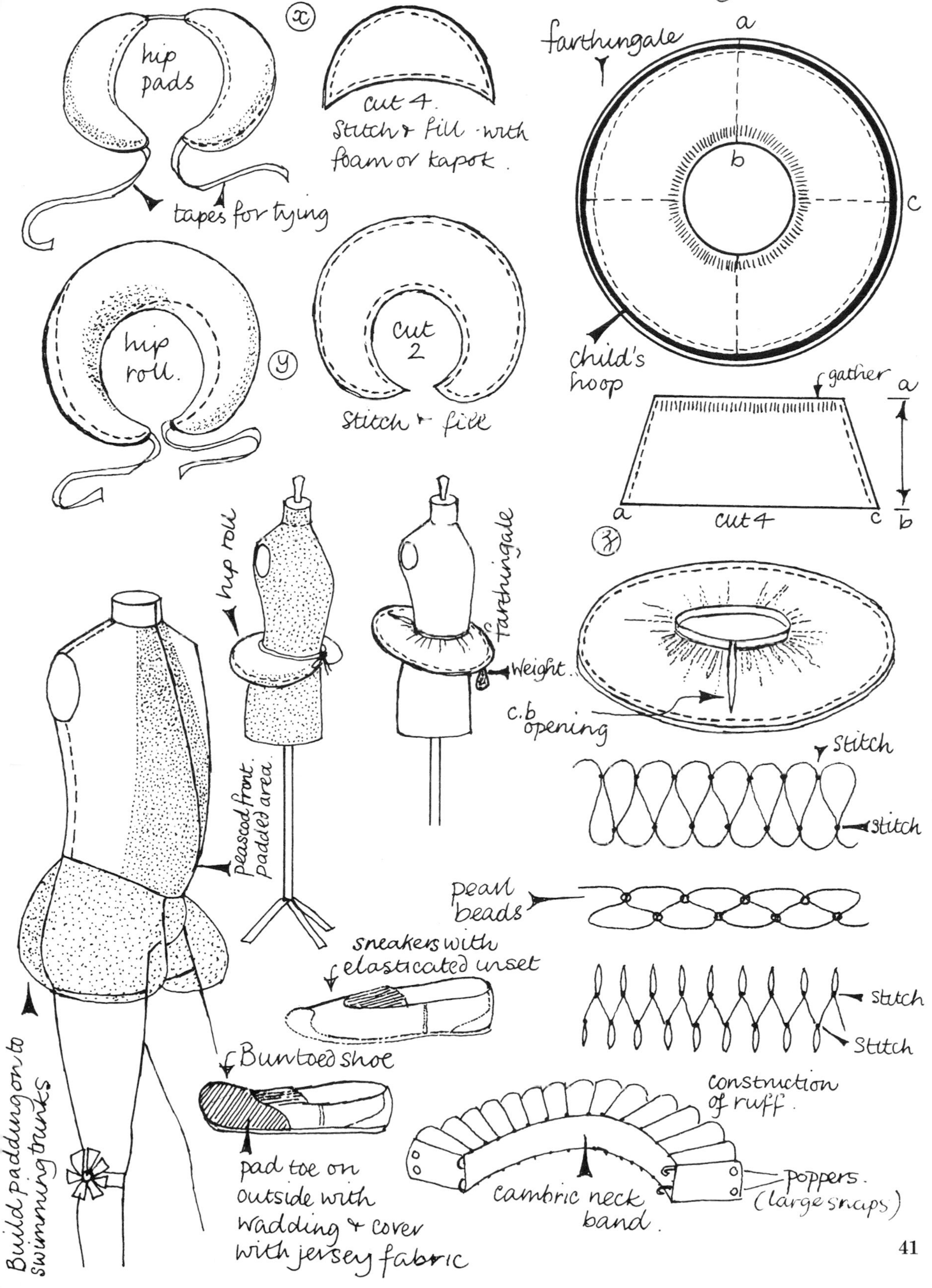

Some C16 Men.

Velvet hat.

sleeves puffed & Slashed

Short cape.

Pair of boots hanging up

Plain linen collar & cuffs

tunic with basque

early C16

Cobbler wearing an apron.

gauntlet gloves

medallion worn on ribbon

puffed breeches

tights

ruff

collar

Countryman dancing

Cod-piece

42

C16 Women

wimple or coif.

dress worn over hip roll

apron

Woman going to market

straight of fabric

side seam

Sleeveless coat

c.f.

Townswoman

dignified head·dress

net

under sleeves

front lacing.

apron

Jewel on drapery.

overskirt looped up

under skirt.

grand lady

43

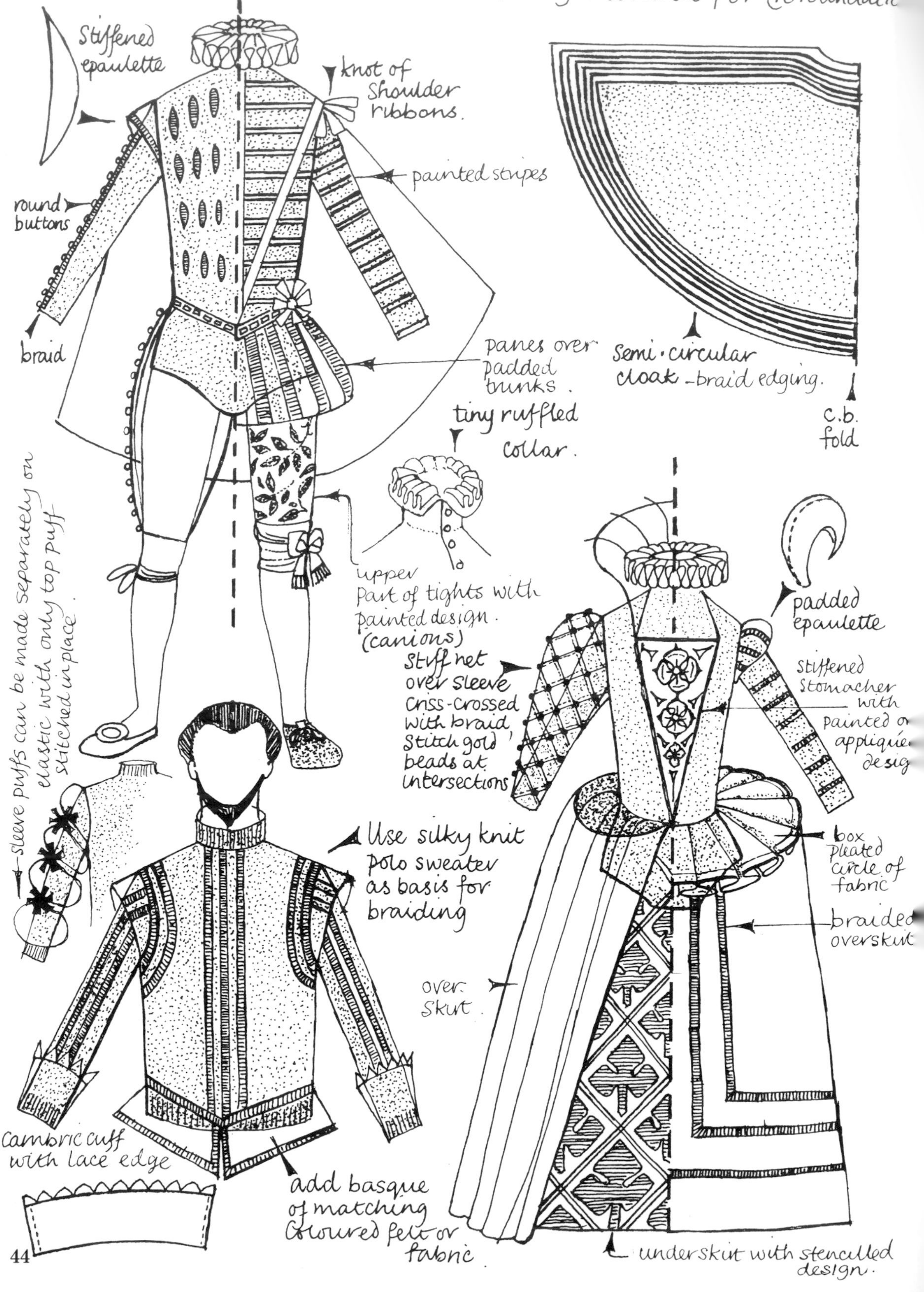

Stiffened epaulette

knot of shoulder ribbons.

painted stripes

round buttons

braid

panes over padded trunks.

semi-circular cloak – braid edging.

c.b. fold

tiny ruffled collar.

upper part of tights with painted design. (canions)

sleeve puffs can be made separately on elastic with only top puff stitched in place

Use silky knit polo sweater as basis for braiding

stiff net over sleeve criss-crossed with braid stitch gold beads at intersections

padded epaulette

stiffened stomacher with painted or appliqué design

box pleated circle of fabric

braided overskirt

over-skirt

Cambric cuff with lace edge

add basque of matching coloured felt or fabric

underskirt with stencilled design

44

7 · The seventeenth century

There is less rigidity in the costume of the seventeenth century than in the previous fifty years – women's dresses are of plain flowing satins and silks rather than the stiff brocades seen before, and ribbons, lace and feathers abound. The influence is strongly Dutch, and the Flemish painters are a useful source of reference. Meticulous paintings by Vermeer, Terborch, Metsu, Steen, Hals come to mind and there are beautiful engravings by Hollar to be consulted. These will form the background for designing costumes for Molière and Congreve, the plays of manners, masques such as *Comus*, and for dramatized versions of *A Pilgrim's Progress*.

A number of ways in which the dress of this period can be adapted by the simplest and most economical means to give the flavour of the time are shown on page 47. Many costumes can be put together by combining everyday garments found in most people's wardrobes with some easily constructed ones, and by the judicious use of detail

For men's waistcoats and breeches use a stout fabric such as felt, canvas or blazer cloth or a firm foam-backed cloth or jersey. Cotton suedette can also be very good. Old blankets can be cut up and are particularly useful for heavy cloaks. All these are excellent for cutting clean shapes and for achieving the boxy outline characteristic of the period. A sweater matched up with an easily-made sleeveless jacket will give the effect of a coat. (See page 50 for patterns.) For a frilly shirt to wear with a be-ribboned bolero, add flounces or frills to ordinary collarless white shirts or to shirts based on the pattern in the eighteenth century section (page 56); soft curtain net can be cut in a circle or semi-circle according to the amount of fullness required, and a cheap lace edging machine-stitched to the outer edge will give a clean finish.

Soft plastic imitation-lace doilies and traycloths will come in very useful. They can be fixed with contact adhesive to tarlatan to make stiff collars for men and women of the first part of the century, and can also be used to make decorative cuffs for boots. Theatrically they are very effective and can be used in many ways to represent expensive lace. Felt, leather-cloth or mock suede can also be used to add bucket tops to boots, and buckles, tongues and bows added to modern walking shoes are a quick and easy way of getting round the footwear problem; they can be easily detachable so as not to spoil the shoes. Gloves can have leather or lace gauntlets added. For more puritanical characters, collars of plain linen can be cut in various sizes. To give them body, use iron-on vilene or staflex interfacing or spray with aerosol starch for a crisp finish.

Round-brimmed dark felt hats, plain for puritans, feathered and be-ribboned for the rich, are universal headgear for men. Hats can also be made on the same principal as the Victorian top hat on page 60, in thick felt stiffened with a proprietary felt-hat stiffener or with shellac painted on with a large brush to give extra body to the felt, and then decorated with tissue paper feathers (see page 114).

For women, basic stays made in a stout elasticated fabric such as that used for bathing costumes or panty-girdles and boned at the side seams will help to give the correct firm, stiff look to the body (see drawing – extra bones can be added if you are ambitious). Over these, sweaters can be worn as a basis for the bodice – silky ones for the aristocracy, woollen or cotton for the middle classes and peasants. They should be close fitting and chosen if possible with a suitable neckline, or can be cut to shape, machine-stitching round the neckline before cutting the knitted fabric to prevent the stitches running, and then trimmed with ribbons – rosettes and bows are both typical – or clusters of pearls to give the right look. Skirts should match the sweaters exactly and be fixed to a waistband or petersham (grosgrain) see page 132. Tabs of the skirt material can be stitched to a belt (see opposite). Skirts are worn over small hip pads. Cuffs and collars follow the same principle as those used for men.

Mules or slippers are common for women; use soft bedroom slippers trimmed with ribbons – or with buckles for outdoor wear. Cloaks and hoods are worn outdoors too. Lace and linen caps are frequently found, often worn under a big felt hat similar in shape to that worn by the men.

For working or going walking the skirt is frequently tucked up in various ways which is very decorative and can show a patterned or gaily coloured petticoat (see particularly the engravings of Hollar). Linen aprons for ordinary people both in and out of doors are worn long, reaching to the hem of the skirt. The skirt itself is frequently braided round the bottom and sometimes down the centre front.

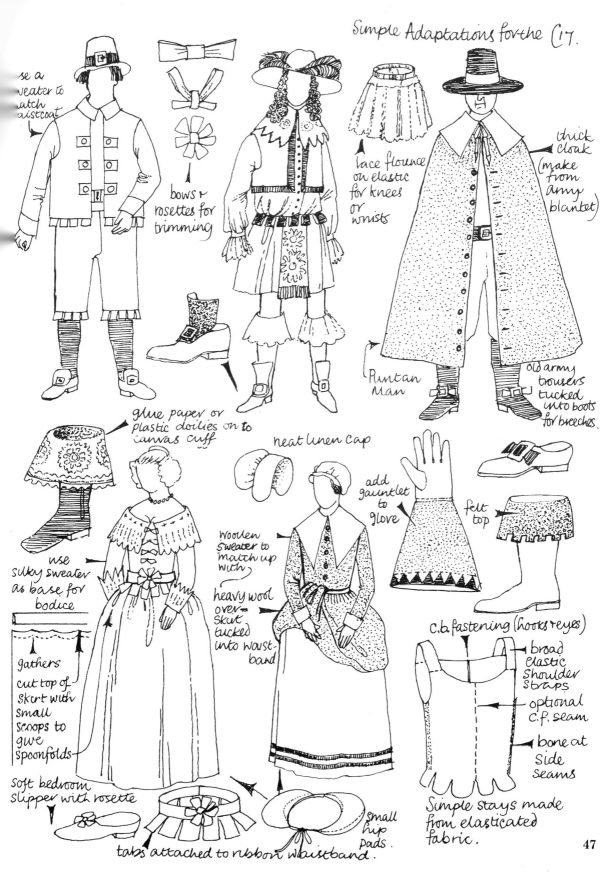

use a sweater to match waistcoat

bows + rosettes for trimming

lace flounce on elastic for knees or wrists

thick cloak (make from Army blanket)

Puritan Man

old army trousers tucked into boots for breeches.

glue paper or plastic doilies on to canvas cuff

neat linen cap

add gauntlet to glove

felt top

use silky sweater as base for bodice

Woollen sweater to match up with

heavy wool over-skirt tucked into waistband

c.b. fastening (hooks & eyes)

broad elastic shoulder straps

optional c.f. seam

bone at side seams

gathers

cut top of skirt with small scoops to give spoonfolds

soft bedroom slipper with rosette

tabs attached to ribbon waistband.

small hip pads.

Simple stays made from elasticated fabric.

Peasant
1668 ▶

cream felt hat ◀

red waistcoat

C17 Men

1646

lace
collar

1635

white
gloves.

Boot &
Shoes.
hanging
in
shoemakers
workshop.

from a
C17 embroidery ◀

armour can be knitted from
dishcloth cotton

48

black jacket with basque

lace cap

brooch

brooch

Well-to-do Puritan mid 17

mule

pearls looped into hair & pearl drop earrings

1635

linen apron

braided hem.

long apron

1660 grand lady in a satin dress

transparent fichu.

from an engraving by Hollar

child wears adult dress in miniature

Woman outdoors with headscarf

note front lacing of simple gown

Middle class woman

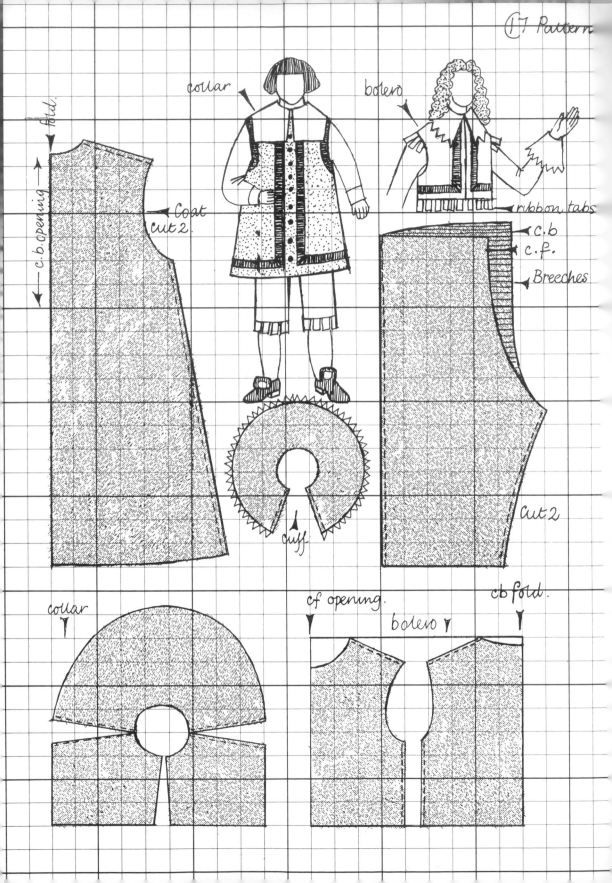

collar

bolero

fold.

← c.b. opening →

Coat
Cut 2.

ribbon tabs

c.b
c.f.
Breeches

Cut 2

cuff

collar

cf opening.

bolero

cb fold.

8 · The eighteenth century

During the first half of the eighteenth century the main influence on costume came from France, where the fashionable life surrounding the court at Versailles and the theatrical extravaganzas performed there were truly magnificent. Smart women were totally obsessed with clothes and in Paris even a humble working woman was dressed very much *á la mode*. Later, English styles predominated; as the country house estate came into its own, simplicity and rusticity prevailed, chintz and muslin replaced silk and satin for the lady, while men's coats were of good cloth and sensible boots replaced elegant heeled shoes.

The man's waistcoat pattern on page 56 is very simple to cut and make.It is suitable for most fabrics from canvas to velvet, but if made in light-weight material it will need lining. Sleeves can be added to the waistcoat pattern to form a coat. The lower part of the centre back seam can be left open to form a vent (shown in the small drawing) as can the side seams – the coat frequently has three vents. For more exaggerated fullness the side seams can be swung out further and pleated at the waist to give the fashionable fan shape shown in the full-skirted coat of 1740. Coat and waistcoat are often of the same fabric but could be different. The waistcoat back is often plain linen whilst the front is rich brocade, cloth of gold or embroidery. Gold and silver lace are frequently appliquéd to the coat; this can be imitated cheaply by spraying an inexpensive lace with gold or silver aerosol spray before sewing or gluing it to the garment. Cuffs vary in size according to the date; to discover what is right for your play, check with the paintings of the period (Hogarth, Gainsborough, Reynolds, Watteau, Fragonard, Boucher, Chardin).

A simple shirt pattern for men is also given on page 56, to be made in soft lawn or muslin so that the fullness typical of the period is soft and elegant rather than stiff and clumsy. The cravat ties round the neck – there are many ways of doing this and again it is well worth consulting the painters before experimenting. The simplest method is to start with the centre of the cravat at the front, wind the two ends round the neck and tie loosely with a knot at the front. The ends of the cravat can be as plain or as lacy and frilled as the character warrants.

Buttons tend to be small but are often jewelled or of cut steel; a plain button can be covered with adhesive and then sprinkled with glittering bugle beads or chopped sequins, and even covering it with silver kitchen foil can have quite a rich effect.

For simulating the breeches of the period, one possibility is to use track-suit trousers or ski-ing pants. These should be cut off just below the knee and finished with a narrow band with a strap and buckle. They are worn with stockings (usually white) rolled over them at the beginning of the century, but later the breeches are pulled over the tops of the stockings.

Highwayman-type capes and cloaks are worn, especially for travelling or for going out at night to revels. A cloak pattern is given on page 61.

Throughout the eighteenth century the tricorne hat, in various sizes, is popular – in fact almost universal. It is basically a round felt hat with the brim curled up in three places (page 55). Sometimes in country districts the curling is ignored. Towards the very end of the century a kind of conical felt hat appears, the forerunner of the top hat which is to become so popular in the years ahead.

In women's dress the hoop again comes into fashion – this time a sideways extension which at its most extreme becomes grotesque. A diagram is shown on page 55 for simple side hoops. Cane, whale-bone or plastic-covered spring curtain wire is run into the slots marked *s* sewn to two panels of fabric worn round the waist on a drawstring. For simple country dresses, side frills of stiff net tied round the waist on the same principal as the hip pads on page 41 will be sufficient. Towards the end of the century the fullness of the skirt is pushed to the back and supported by a bum pad. A complicated corset is beyond the cutting abilities of any but professional dressmakers, but simple stays of elasticated fabric (as described in the previous chapter, page 46) will give a firm shape under a close-fitting nylon sweater with a wide neckline. To this can be added a fichu, lace flounces round the elbows, a lace or embroidered stomacher and other period details. Aprons of various shapes and fabrics are worn to emphasize the fashionable shepherdess look.

In the early 1700's women's heads are small and they wear little muslin caps or straw hats and sometimes rather dashing tricornes. By 1760, however, the fashion is for immense piles of hair, either crowned with silly little hats perched on the front or enveloped in huge organdie mob caps bedecked with lace and ribbons.

Some C18 Men.

note cravat drawn through buttonhole

Samuel Johnson

1760

C18 Theatrical costume — Mr Bensley as Mahomet.

waistcoat

C18 Lamplighter

apron

breeches

hose

bag wig

1780

full skirted coat c.1740. with braided seams.

53

Maid. Servant of the Lady → SAME shape

Straw hat over linen cap

note similarity

pearls. Soft net

lace covered Stomacher

black mittens

gauzy apron.

fichu

rolled up sleeves

lacemaker 1790.

1750

overskirt tucked up at back (sprigged cotton)

buckled shoes

tricorne hat + mask

1750

black lace shawl.

large apron.

Theatrical dress 1778 Mrs Yates as Isabella

gold border. (Spray with gold aerosol through bold lace)

striped petticoat.

brocade skirt - contrive old curtain.

54

sprayed gold + appliqued for rich effect

hessian waistcoat trimmed with cord.

add buckle to Court shoe

fichu

add ribbon bow to mule.

use draw-string blouse

white stockings

add buckles

apron

felt tops to **boots**

man-shoe

breeches from a good engraving

curl edges of round felt hat to make Tricorne

small tricorne

Tricorne

linen cap.

spectacles

felt tongue

eye patch

braided tricorne

Side hoops

Slot for tape

cut 2

1/16 inch = 1 inch

55

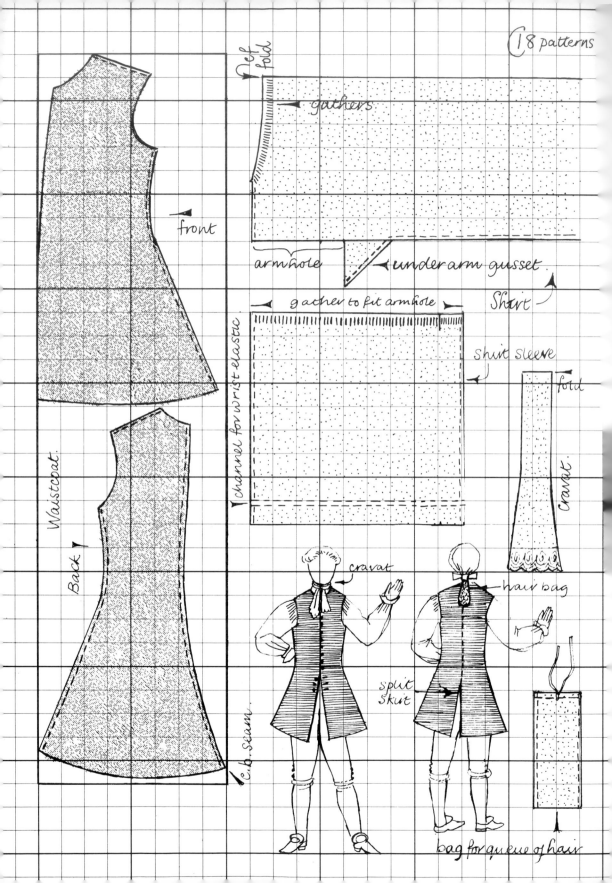

left fold

gathers

front

armhole

under arm gusset

Shirt

gather to fit armhole

channel for wrist elastic

shirt sleeve

fold

Cravat

Waistcoat.

Back

cravat

hair bag

split skirt

c.b. seam.

bag for queue of hair

9 · The nineteenth century

The rural influence is still obvious in men's clothes at the beginning of the nineteenth century, but as the era progresses the general look becomes more urban. This is the beginning of uniformity of colour and style for men, with colours growing more dull as the years pass by. Respectability becomes the hallmark of the man in the street. Beards and facial hair are much in evidence. The top hat becomes almost universal.

Drawings by John Leech in *Punch* magazine are an excellent reference for costumes of this period and the contemporary illustrations to Dickens by Cruickshank and Phiz cannot be bettered for covering a wide cross-section of life.

A certain amount of ingenuity is required to make Victorian clothes on a small budget with simple resources. This is an era of complicated cutting and dressmaking, and the introduction of tailoring in men's garments. Without the help of a tailor an easier way must be found to reproduce the necessary effect. For the man's jacket, a simple method is to braid a slip-over garment as shown in the drawings on page 60, using the pattern on page 61. A smooth foam-backed jersey fabric is excellent for this. If you are using a plain fabric it may be a good idea to paint or stripe it as described in chapter 16, and this is much easier to do before the garment is made up so that the pieces can be laid flat. A silk or wool Russian braid can be used for trimming, but choose one which can easily be manoeuvred round corners and angles. Well-chosen buttons will enhance the effect. Tails can be added to the back of the slip-over to suggest a cut-away coat or tailcoat.

The breeches could also be made from a firm jersey fabric (pattern page 61); a plain colour is most typical. Stitch the centre back and front seams first, then the inside leg seam, and finally the side seams leaving button fastenings at the knee and an opening at one side for a placket. The usual opening for early Victorian breeches and trousers is a drop flap at the front; this can be simulated with a narrow braid.

The cloak pattern can be made any length, with or without the cape. A little extra fullness is desirable at the back, shown on the pattern by the horizontally striped area; this will require a centre-back seam.

Note the variously shaped stiff collars on page 60. These can often be picked up in old-clothes shops; otherwise they can be cut from good quality thin white card and will last for one performance. Stocks and cravats are worn at the beginning of the century but are gradually superseded by the tie. A pattern is given for a top hat. A bowler hat is more of a problem if an old bowler is available the height of the crown can be altered by cutting and gluing, or a papier mâché crown could be built up over a clay mould (see instructions for making masks, page 110). Having built up the clay form, it is worth making a number of crowns and storing them for future use. Always think ahead of ways to save time and effort.

For women, the flimsy, high-waisted classical dress, often cut very low over the bosom and showing the ankles, is popular for the first fifteen to twenty years, reflecting the current laxity of morals. Then, as prudery increases, the great bell skirt begins to swell out, totally concealing from view those unmentionable lower limbs, the legs.

The skirt is at first supported by petticoats, then by hooped crinolines, and later by various kinds of bustle pads, as shown on page 62. To get a good shape it is important that neither the number of petticoats nor the amount of material in them should be skimped. They should be well made and of good quality cotton so that they can be used for many years in subsequent productions.

Page 63 shows some nineteenth-century dresses: (a) a straight-skirted dress of the beginning of the century, (b) and (c) the round bell shape, (d) the soft bustle of the 1860's and (e) the later 'tea-tray' bustle of the 1890's. Page 64 gives ideas for collars and cuffs, many ways of using trimmings, and other details which will help to give character and style. Further details are shown on page 65, with three ways of adapting blouses to easily-made Victorian bodices. The blouses can be fitted to the waist by making tucks or darts, and by lightly boning the bodice at the under-arm seams and the darts under the bust a very neat shape can be achieved; cut the whalebone to the required length, round the ends with a file so that they do not stick through the fabric or into the actress, stitch them into a cotton casing, and fix in place with a herringbone stitch. Make a neat belt of the same colour as the bodice if you want to give the appearance of a longer bodice, or of the skirt fabric if the bodice is meant to be short. Experiment with a number of belt shapes, as they can greatly alter the appearance of the dress.

Footwear consists mostly of dainty slippers or little button boots in soft kid or even satin, suggesting that the Victorian woman did not intend to walk far. Unblocked ballet shoes with small ribbon bows or rosettes added are excellent for this period. Black nylon ankle socks worn over slippers, with buttons or braid stitched up the sides, will produce a neat looking boot.

Gloves are always worn out of doors and are *de rigeur* for evening dress – the fashion plates show pale colours for evenings, on plump rounded arms, with frequently a gold bangle at the wrist. For daytime there are kid, silk and cotton gloves in pale colours and black or brown; lace gloves and mittens are also popular. The shawl is seen everywhere, indoors and out, for both day and evening wear, made of wool, silk, lace or cashmere; for the first three decades it tends to be a long shape, later it is square, folded diagonally. Bonnets are more often seen in the first half of the century; the popularity of hats comes later. Most accessories are small – tiny parasols and fans and, after the early years of the century, neat little muffs. Lockets and cameo brooches are very popular.

On page 93 there is a colour illustration of a selection of fabrics suitable for nineteenth-century costumes.

Some C19 Men

short boxy jacket, with concealed buttons.

apron

canvas gaiters.

Market porter

fur collar

1808 Le Beau Monde

solar topee for explorers & travellers

Seaside Styles.

soft topped cap.

Nov 1839

from Le Follet Courrier des Salons. Waisted coat.

cloth top boots 1860

59

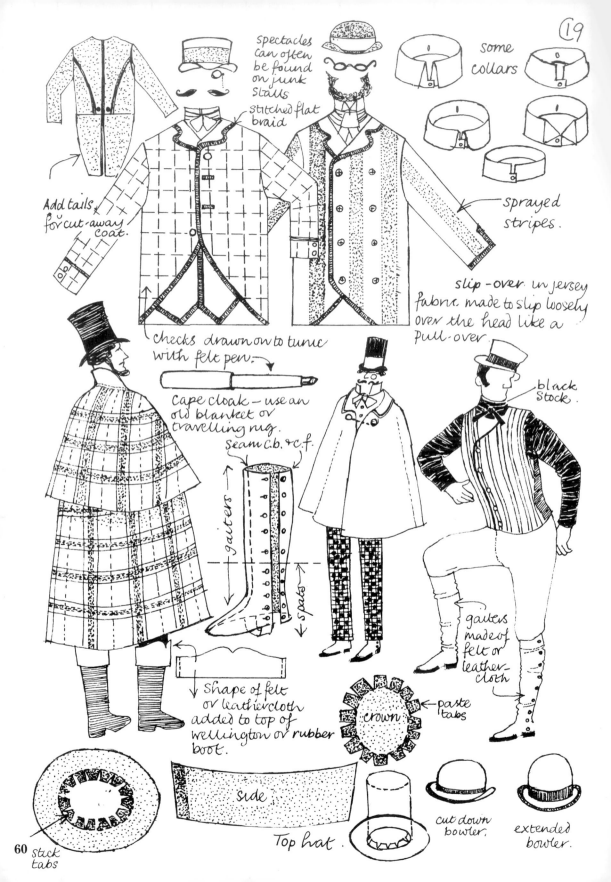

spectacles can often be found on junk stalls

stitched flat braid

some collars

sprayed stripes.

Add tails for cut-away coat.

slip-over in jersey fabric made to slip loosely over the head like a pull-over.

checks drawn on to tunic with felt pen.

Cape cloak – use an old blanket or travelling rug. Seam c.b. & c.f.

black stock.

gaiters

spats

gaiters made of felt or leathercloth

Shape of felt or leathercloth added to top of wellington or rubber boot.

crown

paste tabs

Side

Top hat.

cut down bowler.

extended bowler.

stick tabs

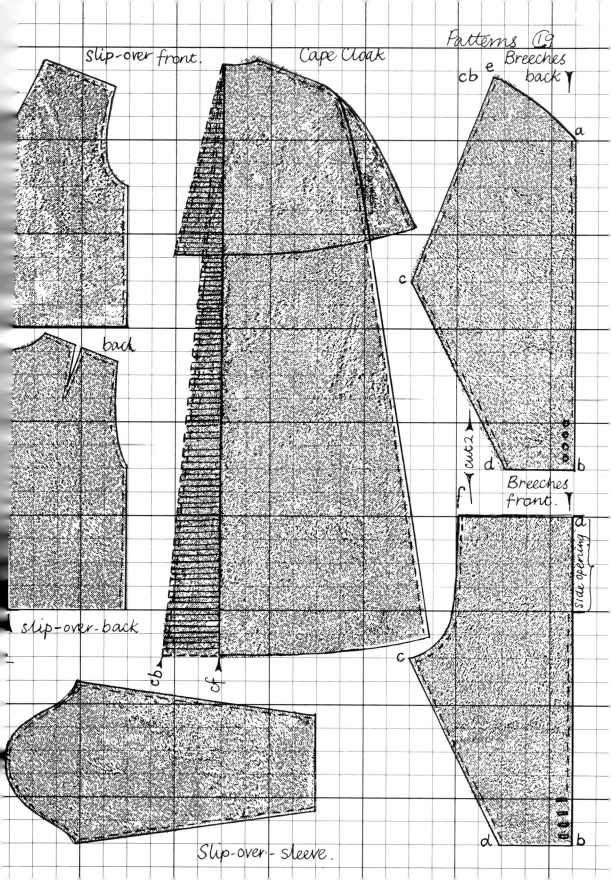

slip-over front.

Cape Cloak

Patterns 19

Breeches
back

cb e

a

back

c

cut 2

d

b

f

Breeches
front.

slip-over-back

a

side opening

cb

cf

c

d

b

Slip-over-sleeve.

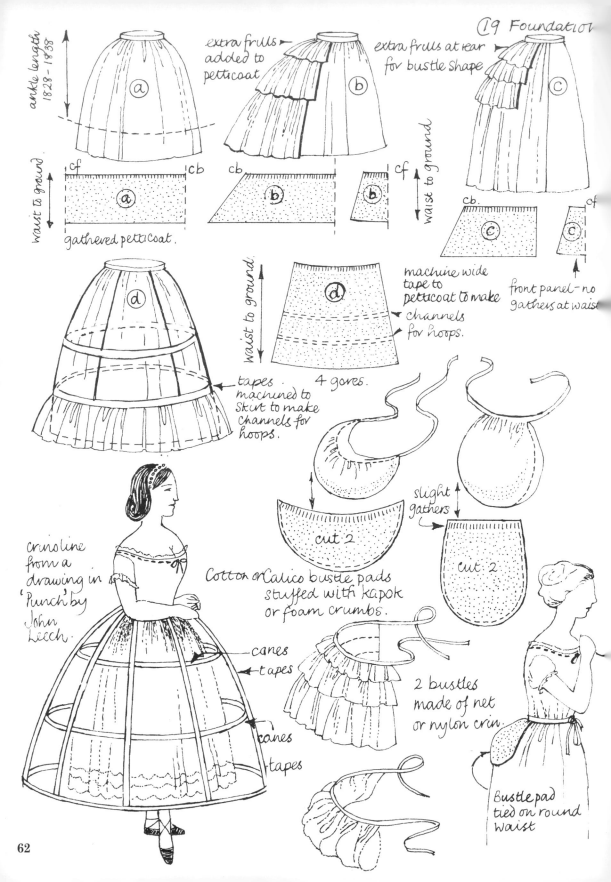

ankle length 1828 – 1838

waist to ground

gathered petticoat.

cf   cb
(a)

extra frulls added to petticoat

cb   cf
(b)   (b)

extra frulls at rear for bustle shape

(c)

waist to ground

cb   cf
(c)   (c)

front panel – no gathers at waist

waist to ground

(d)

machine wide tape to petticoat to make channels for hoops.

4 gores.

(d)

tapes machined to skirt to make channels for hoops.

crinoline from a drawing in 'Punch' by John Leech.

canes
tapes

canes
tapes

Cotton or Calico bustle pads stuffed with kapok or foam crumbs.

cut 2

slight gathers

cut 2

2 bustles made of net or nylon crin.

Bustle pad tied on round waist

neck tie

overskirt looped up at each side c.b.

1868 walking dress. ⓐ

2 tiered cape 1838 ⓑ

1812

velvet spencer

⑲ Women ⓐ

silk boots

Braided or embroidered facings

high necked blouse

riding boot 1868

short gloves

silk or kid slipper

pleated skirt.

fur tippet

cloth top boots

ⓒ 1855 Young girl. Walking dress 1889 ⓔ

63

ribbon bow

ribbon leaf trimming.

ribbon trimmed cuff

2 ribbon trimming

19

organdy ruff

straw hat becomes a bonnet when tied or with a scarf

long scarf

cuff

felt froggings

1802 large muff

1802 long straight skirt.

paper flowers

chemisette

From Punch 1851 drawing by John Leech

snood.

triangular shawl.

3 collars

Note hooped petticoat & pantalettes

Ribbon waist band with attached ribbon trimmings 1868

Crossed fichu — long scarf round back of neck & crossed under belt.

3 adaptations of blouses.

ⓐ lace edging

darts

whalebone

bertha

ⓑ 4 tucks

Bishop Sleeve.

lace jabot

lace motif.

ⓒ ribbon shoulder loops

piping cord spiral on net.

belt shape

c.b.

c.f

c.f

65

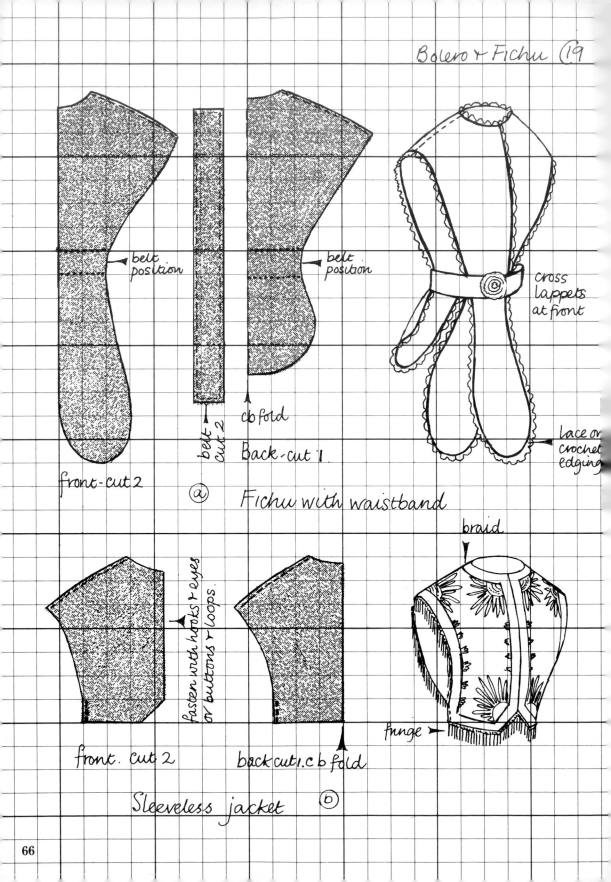

belt position

belt position

belt cut 2

cb fold

Back - cut 1.

front - cut 2

ⓐ Fichu with waistband

cross lappets at front

Lace or crochet edging

braid

fasten with hooks & eyes or buttons & loops.

fringe

front. cut 2

back cut 1. cb fold

Sleeveless jacket ⓑ

The two patterns given here are of details from *The Young English-woman* for 1869. The first is a fichu with a waistband (*a*), consisting of three pieces; it is stitched only at the shoulder seams and is worn over a tight-fitting bodice or blouse. It should be made in a soft wool or silk fabric edged with a narrow lace or crochet or a shallow silk fringe, or could look very decorative in black lace over a white dress. The shape can also be used as a pattern for a crocheted fichu, using either wool or silk crochet thread. Cover the fastening of the belt with a crocheted rosette or a rouleau of fabric.

The second pattern (*b*) is a sleeveless jacket, again to be worn over a blouse or bodice. Make it in firm woollen cloth or cotton velvet. Cut the three pieces as shown, join the shoulder seams and approximately 2in of the under-arm seam at the waist. Fasten at the front with concealed hooks and eyes or button closely with gold buttons and braid loops. The drawing shows the jacket braided in gold, with gold corded sunburst designs, the whole edged with fringe.

The inclusion of a short section on Victorian melodrama seems sensible at this point. These plays were very popular during the nineteenth century, and were much popularized by the 'penny plain, tuppence coloured' prints of Pollock, Skeffington and others. The characters were always very stilted – good and evil were clearly distinguished to create a world split between heroes and heroines and villains. Suitable music accompanied these dramas (as in the days of the silent movies), and the audience booed and hissed the wrong-doers vociferously. These plays make excellent light-hearted entertainment today, and the exaggeration of character makes them fun to dress.

For the well-to-do heroine, the sugary prettiness of the Victorian fashion plate will furnish some ideas; there is no need to spare the flowers, feathers and ribbon bows. For the good young woman fallen on bad times through villainy or the misfortunes of fate, a plain simple dress with a neat lace collar, a clean apron and a plain shawl and lace cap will look right. If she is out of doors – perhaps trudging through the snow with a baby in her arms – a large, all-enveloping shawl is a good choice, covering both mother and child. For poor street characters – crossing sweepers, flower sellers, match girls, etc. – look at Henry Mayhew's books on *London Life* and *The London Poor* which contain both prints and vivid verbal descriptions. Shawls, worn rough coats, battered hats, thick broken-down skirts can be used with tattered blouses and thin ragged aprons. Make mittens from old woollen gloves. Old army boots and beaten-up carpet slippers will come in useful.

Another typical character is the black-cloaked, be-whiskered villain with broad-brimmed felt hat, or sometimes a shiny, insect-like topper; use leather or rubber boots, tucking the trousers into them to make breeches. A poetic hero looks well in a romantic shirt with a Byronic collar; a loosely tied black silk scarf adds a dramatic note, and red leather slippers give an air of oriental debauchery.

The uniform for the soldier on his way to or from the wars can be made up from a tight-fitting red sweater trimmed with braid and buttons; black trousers or, even better, slim-fitting ski pants, should have red or white braid lightly hand-stitched down the side seams. Make a pillbox hat from cardboard, to be worn at a rakish angle on the side of the head. Shiny black plastic shoes would be best; failing these, use black sneakers. Black nylon socks worn over any type of sneaker also give a neat foot.

The diagram shows a simple way to make a coal scuttle bonnet from cardboard or buckram: glue the dotted area of *b* to the tabs of the crown, *a*; then glue the dotted area of *c* to the tabs of piece *b*. The bonnet can be painted or, for a more finished and professional job, covered with a thin fabric and trimmed with feathers, ribbons or flowers; attach ribbons to tie under the chin.

Costumes for a Melodrama

loose scarf tied round neck

Villain

man's cap

Young Flower Girl

Widowed Mother

sacking

add braid to red polo sweater

thick woollen socks worn over plimsolls.

Bonnet

ⓐ

knitted or crocheted Shawl

ⓑ   ⓒ

Soldier.

silk or cotton sash

Old Crone

men's boots

add red braid to black trousers

69

10 · From 1895 to the First World War

During this period the lounge suit gradually supersedes the frock coat for men, except for formal occasions when morning coats are worn. Black jacket and striped trousers are almost a uniform for the city business man. Spongebag trousers (small black and white check) are fairly popular. Blazers – navy blue with a braided edge, cream or striped – can be simulated by the braided or painted slip-over garment described in the previous chapter. Straw or boater hats can be worn with these. The stiff collar in various shapes (see page 60) is universal, except occasionally for a cream or white collar-attached sports shirt seen on the tennis court or worn for boating or other sports. Trousers worn on these occasions were sometimes held up by a neck-tie tied around the waist.

The slip-over garment, made in velvet, can be adapted to represent a smoking jacket with the addition of paisley silk or quilted collar and cuffs and some braiding, as shown on page 73.

Servants played an important part in the establishments of the well-to-do at this time. In fact, the clockwork running of the 'downstairs' household was essential to the glamour of 'upstairs' life. For morning and early afternoon the butler wears a white shirt and black tie and black waistcoat, cutaway coat, striped trousers and white cotton gloves, with a black alpaca jacket when working in his pantry. For the evening he wears a black tailcoat, trousers and waistcoat with white shirt, white bow tie and cotton gloves. The footman wears a dark green or blue cutaway coat, horizontally striped waistcoat, black trousers, white shirt and white bow tie and cotton gloves.

This is the time when the mature woman was really appreciated; an ample figure was the ideal, with the emphasis on a full bosom and large hips. Corsets still confine the figure but the heavy bust seems to overflow at the top and the bottom is pushed backwards, resulting in an S-shaped stance and a kind of pouter-pigeon effect. Frills, flounces and jabots of lace help those less liberally endowed, and the bodice is gathered and dips at the front to overhang the waist. From 1910 the hobble skirt is in fashion for a short time. The daytime neckline is high, almost to the ears at the side where it is supported by tiny bones. The evening décolletage is low, but the neck is often encased in a collar of pearls or brilliants, giving much the same effect as the high collar worn during the day.

Hats are worn straight on upswept, puffed-out hair and often laden with birds and great masses of flowers, frothy confections which can be of immense size and sometimes look as though they are to be eaten rather than worn. Fondant colours are popular.

Soft frilly blouses are much in vogue, and the leg-of-mutton sleeve in fashion at the turn of the century (page 78) deflates as the years go by.

Crisp blouses to wear with 'costumes' are also seen. Short capes are worn for both day and evening and feather or net boas (the latter easily copied with yards of gathered net) are considered becoming.

All society ladies needed a maid to look after and lay out their clothes and to dress them. It is significant that during this period the ladies' dresses all fastened at the back, whereas the servants' clothes fastened at the front. Two parlour maid's dresses are shown on page 74 – the morning dress of serviceable colured cotton with detachable stiff collar and cuffs, worn with a plain white apron with straps crossing at the back and buttoned on to the waistband; and the afternoon dress, invariably black, with a white apron trimmed with broderie anglaise (eyelet embroidery) and tied at the back with a bow. The fashionable shape is echoed in the slight fullness gathered into the waistband at the front. The lady's maid wears a dark, neat dress or blouse and skirt, with some of her mistress's cast-offs for best wear when she is fortunate enough to have a few hours off duty.

The pattern on page 78 is for a typical gored skirt, fashionable from about 1895 when it is at its fullest to approximately 1910 when it begins to be fairly straight. Although from then on the style begins to change, it should be remembered that unfashionable and particularly elderly and conservative women will continue to wear this shape of skirt for many years more. Wedding photographs of the early 1920's shows aunts dressed like this, whilst grandmothers still look positively Victorian. The pattern shows two alternatives: either a six-gore skirt or a skirt with two darts on the hips (x and y) in which the distance y–z can be gathered or pleated to fit the waistband at the back. A very small bum pad can be worn to give a slight lift to the back. The angle of the centre back line can be adjusted to give the amount of fullness required. The skirt usually reaches the tip of the toes in front; at the back it may be walking length or, for more formal occasions and extra elegance, it can trail on the ground for several inches. Almost any fabric can be used – serge or flannel for a walking skirt, silk or velvet for dressy occasions, piqué (ribbed) cotton, linen or drill for summer, and lightweight fabrics such as muslin for a garden party; the latter will need to be lined so that they hold their shape. A braided skirt is shown on page 74, and also one cut in three tiers.

There is also a pattern for a leg-of-mutton sleeve, and a belt or waistband which should be stiffened with tiny bones at the sides and centre front.

Valet

straw boater

1902 Sailor Suit.

trouser crease

Striped trousers

Suit 1910.

clergyman

boy's cap.

slippers

smoking jacket with quilted collar + cuffs

Short donkey jacket.

double round collar + tie

pince nez

motoring goggles

white edging inside vest.

monocle

cravat

Motoring Outfit 1910.

appliqué silk revers + braid

white double round collar with striped shirt

striped blazer, V neck pull-over.

Slip-over adapted to Smoking jacket

Gerald Du-Maurier

cream flannels **73**

Cape with ribbon trimming

stiff collar

Silk or velvet bow.

ruffled net frill tied with velvet ribbon

Parasols were very popular

muslin cap with streamers at back

Soft net skirt. (Use curtain net)

long gloves.

braiding

cambric apron with broderie anglais. insertion

stiff collar.

tucked sleeve

Parlour-maid Afternoon dress

Parlour maid - Morning dress

Plain apron stiff collar & cuffs.

74

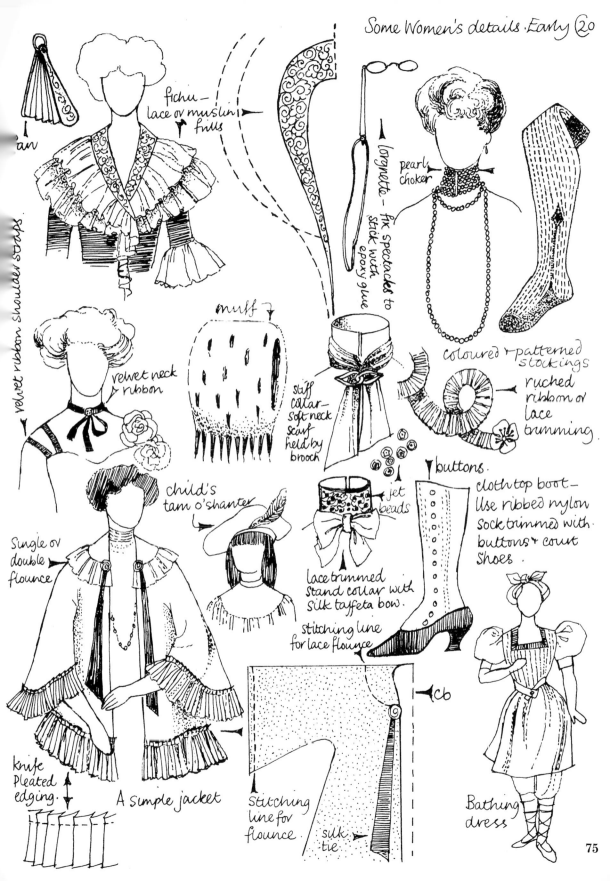

fan

fichu —
lace or muslin
frills

lorgnette — fix spectacles to stick with epoxy glue

pearl choker

velvet ribbon shoulder straps

velvet neck ribbon

muff

stiff collar — soft neck scarf held by brooch

coloured & patterned stockings

ruched ribbon or lace trimming

child's tam o'shanter

jet beads

buttons.

cloth top boot — Use ribbed nylon sock trimmed with buttons & court shoes.

Single or double flounce

lace trimmed stand collar with silk taffeta bow.

stitching line for lace flounce

knife pleated edging.

A simple jacket

stitching line for flounce.

silk tie

cb

Bathing dress

The Music Hall or Vaudeville originated in public houses and bars, where the entertainer was usually a singer. Many of these were eventually taken up by the variety theatres where they were contributed their turns to a long bill of artists. Besides singers and comedians there were conjurors, illusionists, jugglers and male and female impersonators. The costumes of the music hall artists can be seen on the covers of their printed song sheets which show the performer as he or she appeared on the stage.

Because of the unrelated nature of the entertainment, there is no theme of colour or style in a music hall or variety show. The individuality of his act allows the performer to develop his own costume out of his personality and his material. On the whole, there is a tendency for the costume to be an exaggerated or bizarre version of contemporary dress. Some adopt a grotesque style – for instance, Charlie Chaplin with his boots, his over-large clothes, bowler hat and toothbrush moustache, Bud Flanagan in his straw hat and ridiculous fur coat, Little Tich whose big boots exaggerate his minute stature, and Wilkie Bard, the female impersonator.

Some artists change their costume for each number but retain some familiar characteristic – Dan Leno keeps the same make-up, Eugene Stratton his black face, and Charlie Case constantly twiddles his piece of string. Sometimes the outfit changes but the silhouette remains the same, as with G. H. Chirgwin, the White-Eyed Kaffir, who wore an elongated top hat and narrow ankle-length coat in a number of different forms such as the striped version in the drawing.

A music hall evening can give a number of performers with diverse talents a chance to join in. Costumes should be brisk and exaggerated in style. A can-can dancer might well make an appearance – the rather well-built young women in concealing frilly knickers are familiar today from the paintings and posters of Toulouse-Lautrec. The costume shown opposite can be created by using a black sweater for the bodice and adapting the pattern for breeches on page 50 for the drawers; the skirt should be at least a full circle with masses of tarlatan frills on the underside and should be mid-calf length. Use black stockings and shoes, or red stockings and black shoes with cross-lacings up the legs. The other dancer's costume, at the top of the page, could be based on a bathing costume, spangled with sequins or trimmed with black lace; add a frothy net skirt and black or brightly-coloured stockings.

1910

one ribbon strap

Use a bathing costume with added net skirt

Dan Leno

Old frock coat

Check trousers

Principal Boy 1905

velvet tunic with diamanté trimming

tights

Little Tich
note special boots.

Painted cotton coat.

frills on underside of skirt

Can Can Costume

black stockings

Wilkie Bard -
Female impersonator
+ pantomime dame

G.H.Chirgwin
(White eyed Kaffir)

77

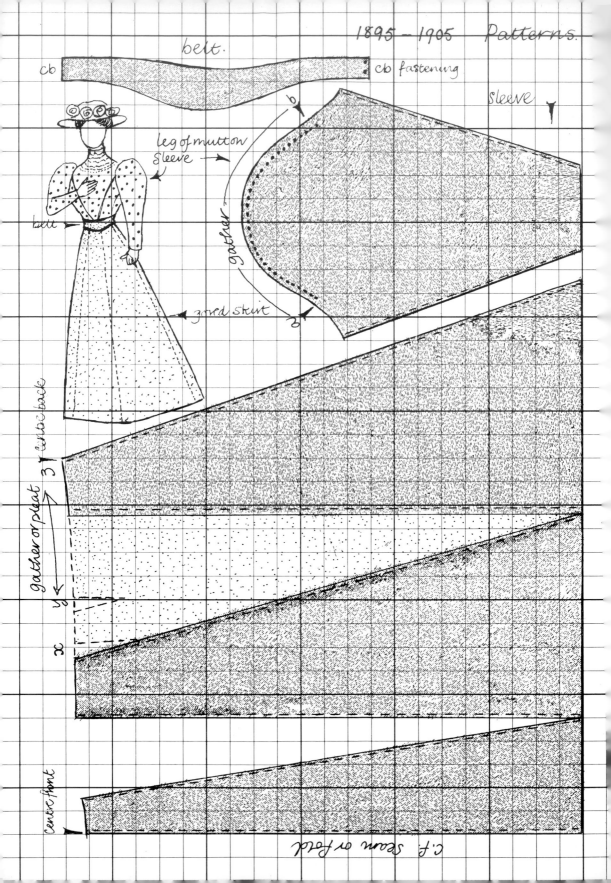

1895 — 1905   Patterns.

belt.

cb   cb fastening

sleeve

leg of mutton
sleeve →

b

gather

gored skirt

centre back

gather or pleat

y

x

centre front

c.f. seam or fold

11 · The twenties and thirties

During this period men's dress becomes more and more relaxed. Suits are for business and town wear, evening dress (and more frequently now the dinner jacket) is for dances and visits to the theatre. There is much emphasis on sport and the smart young man must be correctly dressed for it – sports jackets, blazers, white shirts, cream flannel trousers and fair isle pullovers are all popular. The plus-four suit, first seen on the golf course, is worn for an increasing number of country occasions. The cloth cap also makes its appearance for sport. In both country and town the soft trilby and the homburg hat are commonly worn, the business man is still faithful to his bowler, but the top hat is now becoming the emblem of either a rich man or an undertaker.

The drawings on page 81 show a small cross section of men's clothes of the twenties and thirties. The popular bathing costume of the twenties is most usually of cotton, often in two colours, the part below the waist being black or dark navy; by 1930 a one-colour costume is more common, frequently with two large holes under the arms for sunbathing. The tennis player wears wide trousers known as Oxford bags; these are worn only by the smart set and can vary in width, reaching their widest in 1925; they are worth bearing in mind for the right kind of character in a twenties farce. Spectacles have round lenses with rather narrow tortoiseshell rims. Two-button, three-button and double-breasted suits are all worn; trousers are braced rather high and turn-ups (cuffs) are universal. Ties are narrow, with a small, neat knot and often a tiepin fixing the collar together under the tie. Shirts with a narrow stripe and soft collars have become popular, although the collars are still usually unattached.

During the late twenties and the thirties hiking became an occupation for weekends and holidays, and streams of energetic young people took to the roads in tweed caps and jackets and knee-length shorts; thick ribbed socks, hearty brogues and hairy knees complete the outfit. The golfer also wears a sports jacket and waistcoat with his checked plus-fours; sometimes this is a matching three-piece suit. Note the diamond-patterned socks with flashes at the side of the calf. Two-tone shoes known as 'co-respondents' are sometimes worn.

The emancipation of women brought about by the First World War is by now reflected in their dress. The mature woman has had her day and the Bright Young Thing, the 'flapper', is all the rage. From 1920 skirts begin gradually to rise until in 1927 they reach the knee – an amazing event! Alongside this revolution the bust disappears (those unfortunates who were well endowed bound their breasts to achieve a boyish figure) and the waist drops. Hair is cut short, even shingled, to look like a man's. In the background, the older members of the family still cling to their earlier style of dress with longer skirts and corsets, as can be seen very clearly in *Punch* magazine and other contemporary illustrated periodicals.

The drawings on page 82 show some of the simplest women's clothes. The twenties cut is uncomplicated, but the more sophisticated dresses have inserts and pleats and other details which give some variety to an otherwise very straight shape. Checked, striped and spotted fabrics are used a great deal and there are a great many jumper blouses, either crocheted or knitted in silk. The coat may be edge-to-edge or fastened very low with either one or two buttons, a low belt or a tie. Deep collars are in fashion and for evening wear are sometimes padded or quilted. The large-brimmed hat gives way to the cloche, sometimes completely brimless, which fits closely over the close-cropped head and reaches down to the eyebrows.

Shoes have very pointed toes and 'lavatory' heels and are often in very pale colours, stockings too are light in tone and, combined with the very short skirt, can be rather unflattering to the legs.

The mannish look for women is often heightened by a waistcoat and a collar and tie, or a fair isle pullover. Young women have now really entered the world of sport, and are sometimes seen in shorts when hiking. Tennis dresses are of white silk or piqué. A pleated skirt gives freedom of movement and is worn on a camisole top; the bodice reaches the widest part of the hips where the skirt is attached so that it falls quite straight. This is seen right through the period from about 1920. The shape of the skirt can be varied in many ways – there are two examples on page 83. Also shown is a sleeveless blousette to be worn under a costume or cardigan, provided the jacket is not going to be removed; these are easy to make and variations will help to give a different look to the outfit.

From around 1930 there is a return to more femininity and a gradual softening of the female contour, although without any degree of voluptuousness. Skirts become longer again and are often flared or cut on the bias and clinging, and the waist returns to its natural position. Evening dresses in the thirties are cut very low at the back. Pyjama suits with wide trousers are sometimes seen on the beach or for lounging at home in the evening.

Pattern 1 on page 84 is for the kimono-like wrap or coatee shown on page 83. Cut one piece double with *a–c* on a fold, for the back. Cut two fronts the same shape but cutting along the line *a–c*. Gather *a–g* on the two front pieces until the shoulder seam *a–b* equals the stitching line *b–f*, to give the front fullness shown in the drawing. Paint or appliqué the design on to the flat pieces before joining the shoulder and under-arm seams.

For the dress, pattern 2, cut both pieces double on centre fold. Make tiny pin tucks at the front shoulders and at the low waist; cut and bind the four slots for the sash as marked, before making up. The sash should be cut on the bias, single thickness, in a light material which will drape pleasantly. Cut two pieces (*x*), gather and pleat at both ends and insert in the slots, front and back, and stitch into place. Gather the drape (*y*) at the top, twist into a rosette and fix in place at the side of the sash as shown in the drawing. This pattern can be adapted for other dresses, varying the details, with or without sleeves.

It is well worth searching in junk shops and old trunks in the attic for useful garments of this period.

Tennis player

belt

Tie with small tight knot.

C

2 button suit

Bathing costume 1930

Oxford Bags ➤

double breasted suit

trousers worn rather short (braced high)

Golfer

plus fours

Hiker.

Flannel shorts

braces

tie pin

knitted tie

Patent evening pumps 1920

brogue walking shoes

81

Japanese parasol of oiled paper

charming
river frock

1923

Dress &
coat with
matching
lining.
1927

Waistcoat
1927

For the bea

child's
sunbonnet
1923.

style for tennis

coat
with
typical
1927
collar

1938
Beach
Outfit.
Halter neck
sun top &
wide trouse

mid 1930's

court shoes.

lavatory
heel

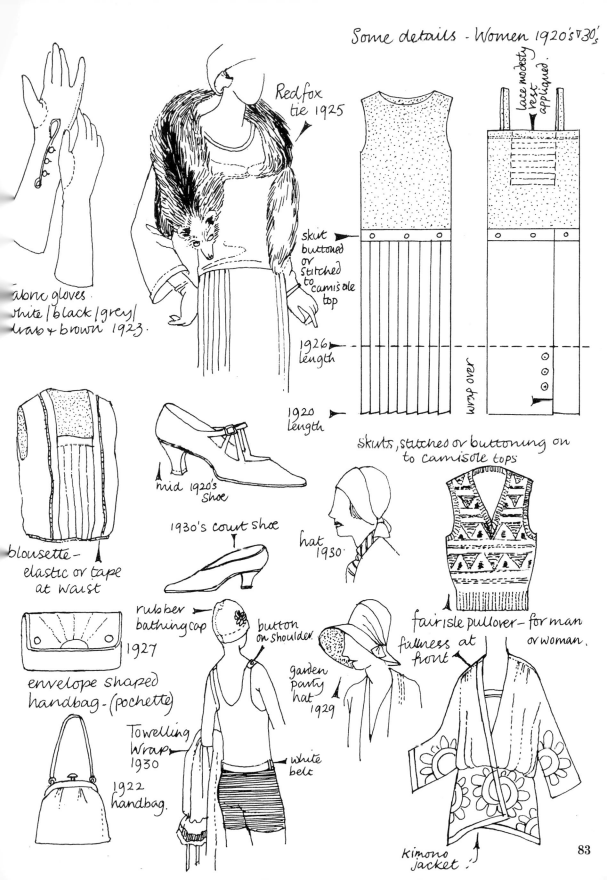

Red fox tie 1925

lace modesty vest appliqued.

fabric gloves white / black / grey / drab & brown 1923.

skirt buttoned or stitched to camisole top

1926 length

1920 length

wrap over

skirts, stitched or buttoning on to camisole tops

mid 1920's shoe

1930's court shoe

hat 1930

fairisle pullover- for man or woman.

blousette- elastic or tape at waist

rubber bathing cap

button on shoulder

fullness at front

envelope shaped handbag- (pochette)

1927

garden party hat 1929

Towelling Wrap 1930

white belt

1922 handbag.

kimono jacket.

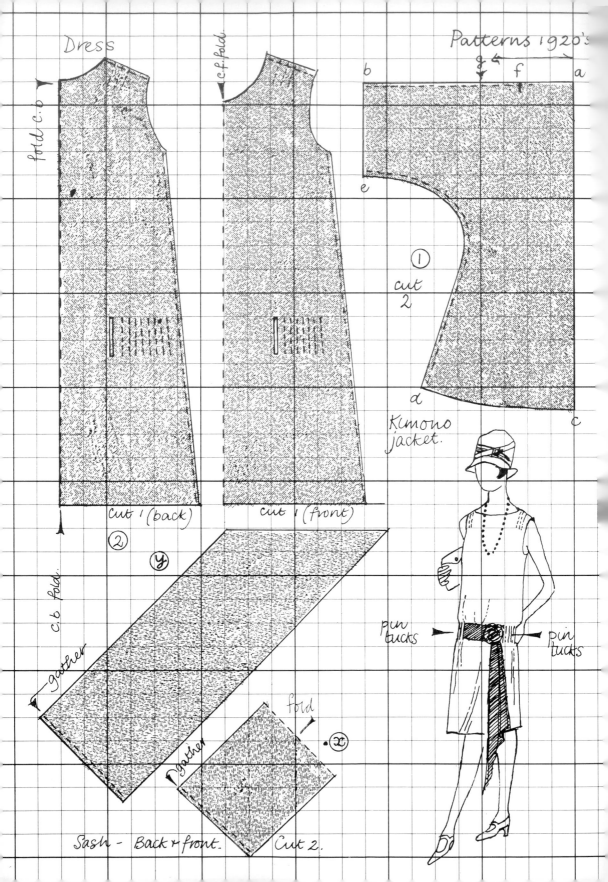

Dress

c.f. fold

Patterns 1920's

fold c.b

b   f   a

e

① cut 2

d

c

Kimono jacket.

cut 1 (back)

cut 1 (front)

② ⓨ

c.b fold.

gather

gather

fold

ⓧ

Sash - Back + front.   Cut 2.

pin tucks

pin tucks

12 · Yesterday and today

With the end of the 1930's the frivolities of the between-wars period which had been reflected in dress once again disappeared as clothing became more serviceable and business-like. With the return of wartime restrictions people were forced to have fewer clothes. Skirts, which had dropped to low calf length by 1939, began to creep up again until they reached the knee; trousers, previously confined to Bright Young Things, were now worn by increasing numbers of women for both warmth and convenience. Colours, on the whole, were rather drab, reflecting perhaps the fact that few women had time to think much about clothes and men of an age to be clothes-conscious were in uniform. Pixie hoods, headscarves and eventually turbans (originally worn as a safety measure by factory girls) made their appearance on the heads of women of all classes. With the introduction of clothes rationing in some countries, ingenuity was at a premium – blouses were made from dusters, capes and cloaks from blankets, and it was discovered that two studded dog collars buckled together made a chic belt. For summer days, leg paint in various shades of tan could be bought from the chemist as a substitute for stockings

With the return of peace the informality which had characterized wartime continued. Formal dress was no longer insisted on for theatre visits and social functions, the days when every smart man must have a dinner suit had gone for good.

People in jobs which had previously required a uniform, such as postmen and public transport workers, complied less and less with the regulations. Bank clerks, office workers and professional men who had always worn formal suits now became more relaxed in their choice of clothes. Curls and whisps of hair appeared from under nurses' caps, even nuns gradually abandoned their centuries-old medieval habits and showed their ankles.

In an effort to break away from uniform and express themselves, young people began in a strange way to look curiously alike in their universal denim blue jeans, T-shirts and longer hair, so that the sexes became difficult to distinguish.

The field of fashion has now broadened considerably and is available to practically everyone, not just the fortunate wealthy few as was once the case, so that dress has become increasingly standardized in all walks of life. Moreover, with the very transient nature of fashions today, garments have become much more expendable. The shortage of natural fibres – wool, silk and cotton – and improved technology have gradually led to the widespread use of synthetics in every field and these, in their turn, have affected today's dress. Some synthetic fabrics are still difficult to handle from a dress-making point of view and some are uncomfortable to wear.

The planning of costumes for modern plays follows the same pattern as for other productions, although it will in most cases be a process of selection and adaptation rather than designing and making from scratch. This need not make the task any less interesting, as attention must still be paid to the choice and balance of colour, the use of plain fabrics contrasted with patterns and of contrasting patterns used side by side. Use can also be made of interesting textures and weights of fabric.

Sometimes costumes can be built up from the actor's own wardrobe, otherwise it may be necessary to beg or borrow from friends and relations or to adapt and add to what is available. This is a time when different age groups can contribute, when grandparents and aunts may be asked to delve into their wardrobes, and trunks tucked away in lofts and cellars should be investigated. Specific outfits, such as academic and legal robes, nurses' uniforms and clerical dress can probably be borrowed locally. Second-hand clothes shops and flea markets are worth exploring for possible bargains. Building up a character by putting together the right garments calls for a special kind of skill which includes keen observation of one's fellow human beings.

13 · Underwear and nightwear

As I have already shown, certain under-garments are often necessary to give costumes the correct shape. The clothes on the next two pages are not, however, 'foundation' garments but are included because they may be helpful for bedroom scenes requiring a certain amount of undress. In pantomimes, too, there is generally an undressing scene for the Dame; and such items as pantalettes and chemises can form a pretty basis for a line of dancers in a musical or variety show.

With the exception of the occasional red flannel petticoat and the use of black lace for fast women and Guy de Maupassant prostitutes, underwear was usually white, though in the 1920's pale pinks, blues and coffee colours became popular. Lawn and fine cotton are suitable fabrics, trimmed with broderie anglaise (eyelet embroidery) and lace, fastened with drawstrings, tapes and ribbons and cotton buttons. The earliest form of pantalettes consisted of two separate legs on a tape round the waist, but this is hardly suitable for the stage! A later, one-piece form is shown here. Contrary to the chocolate-box image of Victorian ladies, pantalettes rarely showed below the dress. Combinations were frequently worn by Edwardian ladies. Until well into the twentieth century, underwear was not usually very revealing and was worn for warmth – just as night-caps were originally worn to keep the head warm in bed, although by the 1920's they began to serve the purpose of holding the Marcel-waved hair in place and were made dainty with laces and ribbons.

Dressing gowns range from sensible woollen or quilted garments to frilly peignoires and, from Edwardian times, the use of Japanese kimonos, either real or copied. Shawls were also worn in the bedroom or in bed. Glamorous silk dressing gowns for men were made popular by Noel Coward and were almost a uniform for plays of that era and for the farces which were popular in the first three decades of the twentieth century. Pyjamas were worn in the last decade of the nineteenth century but did not really supersede the nightshirt until after 1900.

When making underclothes to be worn under dresses, it is most important that they should be of a fabric which does not create static electricity. This is a great problem with modern synthetic fabrics and should always be borne in mind. If the problem should arise after a garment has been made it can be rinsed in (or sprayed with) one of the antistatic products now available. It is sometimes necessary to treat tights in the same way.

Another important point is the ease with which dressing gowns and negligées will slip on and off; designs which have small armholes or a multitude of fastenings should be avoided. A loose tie belt is easiest to fasten and unfasten; hooks and eyes and buttons should not be too small or inaccessible; tapes and ribbons very easily become knotted. Actresses do not want to have to concentrate on these details. Sometimes two small pieces of velcro disguised by a bow will save a terrible hassle. Slippers, too, must slip on and off easily – mules present the fewest problems.

night cap

victorian pantalettes

Victorian nightdress

1928

Slumber helmet 1928

embroidery

scalloped edging

boudoir cap.

dressing gown of wool backed satin

late victorian petticoat with train

mule.

Flannelette nightgown

camisole

Slipper

felt slipper

88

Early C18 chemise made in cotton

lace.

lace

lace tie

braid

back view

viyella dressing gown

Combinations. (Elastic woollen texture) 1890's

petticoat 1927

Dressing Jacket 1912

shawl collar in satin

Man's silk diamond patterned dressing gown. 1936

14 · Stylization

The style in which a play is to be produced and performed is decided by the director after reading and working on the script and reaching a clear idea in his own mind of what he and the play are trying to say and the best way to set about it. At this point, a discussion must take place with the set designer, the costume designer and the lighting designer so that they all understand one another from the start, pool their ideas and work together to get a unified production. It is necessary that all these people should keep one another fully informed at every stage and support one another in all difficulties and problems.

There are very few plays which cannot be presented in a stylized way. It should be understood that style and stylization are two entirely different things: for instance, the style of eighteenth-century costumes means something quite different from the stylization of eighteenth-century costumes. The 'style' is the combination of general appearance, shape and manner of wearing the clothes of the period. To make a 'stylized' version of those clothes is to select, present and prune certain aspects of them, to point and emphasize particular characteristics, and in some cases to simplify or modify.

Stylization can lead to a cheaper way of presentation (though in no way a poorer one) by using very simple shapes and a few well-chosen and well-designed details. Conversely, it can lead to more expense as it may mean less utilization of existing resources and more cost in procuring and making everything from scratch. This can easily happen if a decision is made to limit the colour range of the costumes – as, for example, in creating a production entirely in black and white, or when selecting a limited range of colours for a specific effect. A production may be planned in glowing golds, reds, oranges and hot browns to suggest heat or passion, or in cold colours for a grim, northern feeling. It will then be necessary to buy or to dye fabrics to fit the chosen colour range.

A very stylized approach can be achieved by the extensive use of painted design on costumes, employing bold brushwork on simple canvas shapes. The paper sack costumes described in the chapter for schools (page 133) are an example of this idea carried to its extreme. This method demonstrates how stylization is controlled by the limitations of the materials and also shows how such limitation can unify the visual effect. It is an idea which can be expanded into the area of fabrics and simple shapes when approached with simplicity and wit.

Basing a set of costumes on T-shirts and tights, or leotards, or sweaters and trousers, to give anonymity of colour, and then adding to each performer some particular feature which brings out the most salient aspect of his role, is an interesting and challenging form of stylization. These details must be designed and chosen with the utmost care and the choice of colour and proportion must be exactly right, for they will become important visual symbols. The same kind of basic costume could be used for a production using only beautifully designed and made paper hats, or papier mâché masks or heads.

Designing costumes to put before a plain backing such as curtains or a cyclorama makes great demands on the imagination and capabilities of the designer. In a situation where the facilities for making or painting scenery are limited, this may be the only solution if a production is to be mounted at all. A telling silhouette becomes essential. Remember that the attention of the audience will be focused entirely on the characters and an enormous reponsibility rests on the costume designer to create not only the costume for each actor/character but also the mood of the scene and the play.

Some stylization arises out of the physical needs of the performer – a constant problem for the designer and maker of dancers' costumes, where everything must be considered in terms of freedom of movement. Time spent looking at professional designs for ballet and also the specialized costumes worn by circus acts will be amply repaid. Look also at photographs of the Japanese Theatre, African dance groups and even at some really good puppet productions; see particularly *Play with Light and Shadow* by Herta Schönewolf, which has some very inspiring photographs. Always look at the best, even if you are only an embryo designer – some of the gold dust of the really good designer will rub off on you.

All these uses of stylization demand the co-operation of the performer, for the costumes must be worn in a way that will contribute to and enhance their effect and this requires understanding. The actors will need to get used to the idea of the costumes and to enjoy wearing them.

15 · Thinking about colour

A number of factors govern the selection of colours for a production – the mood of the play, its geographical situation (which to a certain extent dictates what kind of lighting – bright, dim, warm, cold – will be thrown upon it), the historical period in which the piece is set, and the class of society it describes. The ideas of the producer, set designer and costume designer must be fully discussed and sorted out, with a breakdown of scene changes and costume changes. Changes of mood and the various dramatic climaxes need to be decided upon so that thought can be given to tonal and colour groupings and accents of intense pure colour which will be used to heighten certain moments.

FABRICS FOR NINETEENTH-CENTURY COSTUMES

The cuttings shown opposite will give an idea of fabrics and colours suitable for nineteenth-century plays.

a Black lace over silky-finish cotton – very decorative in effect.

b, c Checks for shirts, jackets, or for facing on men's slip-over jackets (p. 60); *f1* and *f2* show the two sides of a cotton jersey fabric particularly suitable for these slip-overs, and the striped cotton (*v*) could be used for detail or for striped sleeves to give the effect of a waistcoat.

d, k, l, p, r and *w* Light cotton prints, suitable for pretty, early Victorian dresses.

e Printed velvet for a flamboyant cloak, wrap or jacket, or for showy trimmings.

i and *j* Darker cotton prints, for prim elderly ladies throughout the century.

g A black and white stripe which would make a striking dress.

h, q A cotton check and a striped cotton lawn, both good for seaside dresses of the 1860's and 1870's.

m, n Embroidered nylon, and a spotted fabric, for thin summer dresses.

o Furnishing velvet, for a cloak or muff.

s Printed needlecord for capes, cloaks and jackets.

t Printed viyella (wool and cotton) – rather expensive for a dress, but scraps can be used for cuffs, collars, revers, etc.

u Suitable for a wrap or pelerine with a plain lining, edged with braid or fringe.

   For a broader and more theatrical effect, these patterns could provide inspiration for painting, spraying and printing fabrics.

Before starting on the designs it is advisable to invest in some good quality paper and to stretch it: wet it thoroughly with clean warm water, drain it for a moment or two, then lay it on a drawing board and secure it to the surface round the edges with gummed paper tape (*not* Scotch tape), overlapping the paper about ⅜in. Dry in a warm atmosphere, but not before direct heat or the paper may pull away from the board. A tinted paper (such as Ingres paper) or a colour-wash background will help to create the mood of the backing. Watercolours, inks, gouache colours, oil pastels and acrylics are all suitable media – either alone or in combination.

Set out your characters quite small, grouped together as they will appear in the various scenes through the play. Quite simple blobs of colour can convey the characters, shapes and patterns you intend to use. If a character does not look right first time, or even second or third time, it can be sponged out with a soft sponge and clean water and, after the paper has dried, can be redrawn in the same position. Should the surface of the paper eventually become useless with washing out or erasure, a small piece of fresh paper can be fixed in place and the character redrawn without interfering with the layout of work already satisfactorily achieved.

Plan a theme of colour to run throughout the play, limiting or broadening it according to the development of the scenes. There needs to be some kind of relationship between all the colours and characters – even the clashing ones. When mixing your colours, add a little of a colour you have already used to the next colour – this will give a basic unity; then, here and there, a heightened note of pure singing colour can be added to accent a character or a dramatic point.

If, when you begin to plan the fabrics for the designs, dyeing, painting and spraying seem desirable the same procedure can be applied to this stage of the work. Choose a clear mid-tone colour for the first length of fabric so that different dyes can be added to the original dye bath for subsequent pieces, thus giving the colour link already worked out in the design. (See chapter 16 for advice on dyeing, etc.)

FINALIZING THE COSTUME DESIGNS

When the preliminary costume plan is complete, arrange a further discussion with the director to lay before him the ideas you have succeeded in putting on paper. When any final changes have been agreed upon you can start work on a set of costume plates, working from your first groups of characters.

This is the time to search for fabrics in the colours, patterns and textures you require. You will be lucky if all the exact colours are available, but it is often possible to achieve what you have in mind by putting the fabric through a thin dye which will either dull or slightly alter the original colour. Some patterned fabrics need extra painting or printing, either changing the scale of the pattern or adding a further colour to get nearer to your design. A light spray of paint or dye is also helpful in colour adjustment. Bear in mind that colours can look quite different under theatrical lighting compared with their appearance in daylight or the fluorescent lighting often used in shops. Under bright lights pale colours can appear very bleached out; and if the lighting is dim there will be very little difference of colour in the darker tones. In either situation pure white can jump out of the stage picture, so whites may need to be sprayed down or dipped at the last moment to get something which blends harmoniously.

The finished costume plate must explain absolutely clearly your intentions with regard to the final costume and should include notes and diagrams when necessary. Cut small patterns of the fabrics and trimmings to be used and attach them to the sketch. If you have access to a photocopying machine, extra copies are always useful – one can go to the prop jeweller or to the hat maker; as these copies will be in black and white, pin fabric samples to them too, making quite plain which fabric is used for which part of the design. With some costumes there are bound to be colour adjustments due to unavailability of fabrics, cost problems, etc. As long as the alternative colour or shade works well within the framework of the overall plan for the production, a few alterations here and there will not damage the total look.

There is less room for manoeuvrability in a stylized colour production when only a very restricted range is being used. A wrong tone or slightly 'off' colour can upset the whole balance of a design or even of a complete production. In this case it is usually wiser to decide on the range of fabrics with the producer before starting work on the designs.

Remember that all items are important colourwise and that the hat or head-dress, shoes and all other details (umbrella, gloves, fan, etc.) contribute to the complete costume which in its turn is an important part of the entire picture.

TRIMMINGS

A selection of braids, trimmings and motifs is set out on page 101, giving some idea of the possibilities in this field. The market is of course constantly changing and the invention of new materials and synthetic fibres increases the selection every day.

True period trimmings from the past can frequently be found on junk stalls and, while searching for these, lace, buttons and artificial flowers can sometimes be picked up. Period dresses which have perished and are of no further use frequently have braid and lace still with life in them which can be unpicked. Do not regard braid as a finite thing – two or three varieties can be used together, or beads, threads, wools, sequins etc. can be incorporated with them. Braid can be threaded through coarse lace, or lace can be laid over braid. Experiment with twisting, knotting and plaiting. Use paint for dulling down trimmings so that they will blend with a costume; conversely, bright paint will help to emphasize or pick out a trimming when this is required. Braid can be used for creating stripes or lattice patterns and for outlining and emphasizing shapes and seams or for edging garments. It may be cut up to build decorative designs for stomachers, bodices or tunics, or can be used to emphasize button holes and to make either simple or complicated frogging for the fastenings of coats and cloaks.

Fringes and tassels, not shown in the illustration, have similar uses.

Layout of cartoon strip of characters to show colour & shape relationship
Colour back ground used to suggest colour of set & low key lighting.

Note use of small areas of glowing colour contrasting with general gloom.

Coloured
Stitched
Straw shape

pleated drape
over light foundation

thick white
piping cord

white
pulp thing balls

felt appliqué
continued down
back of coat

paper
pulp
beads

Shirt
material

patterned
cotton shirt

Sashes in 2
colours of
Jersey.

striped
cotton coat

pink
cotton sateen
turkish trousers

Jersey
for
sashes

cotton pulp
ball stitched on
appliqué for
3 dimensional
effect

↑
Cotton Sateen
dip in yellow dye to
get a more salmon pink colour

J. Shear –
An Arabian Night

Draw final costume plates clearly + as simply as possible
to aid maker in following the design. Full consultation with
the maker is essential

16 · Fabrics, plain and patterned

It may not always be possible to buy fabrics you can afford in the colours and patterns you need for a particular costume or play, so dyeing and painting inexpensive fabrics or old sheets, blankets or curtains will be the answer. In this way it is also possible to unify an assorted collection of existing garments into a well-planned ensemble or to create an overall scheme for a whole production.

DYEING

It is important to have suitable facilities for dyeing: a large zinc dye bath is required for all but the smallest articles, for without it results are likely to be erratic; the material must be boiled, which entails the use of an electric ring or gas burner; a sink with running water facilitates matters, and somewhere for hanging the material to dry must be available. A sturdy stick for agitating the material and a pair of tongs for lifting it out of the bath will also be needed and rubber gloves will protect your hands. It is a great help to have the assistance of another person when lifting heavy wet material out of the dye bath. Large items can also be dyed in a washing machine; follow the instuctions given in the dye package.

Be sure everything is to hand before starting. Do not try to economize over the amount of dye used; use a commercial variety such as Dylon (Rit or Tintex in the US) which is cheap and reliable, and follow the quantities recommended. These dyes can be mixed to obtain the required colour.

Fill the dye bath with water and set it to boil, adding two tablespoons of salt; meanwhile mix the dye powder with a little hot water. When the water in the dye bath is hot, pour in the dye and stir thoroughly. Make tests with scraps of fabric until a satisfactory colour is obtained.

Soak the material to be dyed in a sink full of water, then lower it into the dye bath. Bring to the boil, agitating it all the time with the stick until the colour is strong enough, then lift it out and put it into the sink. Rinse with plenty of cold water, squeeze but do not wring out, and finally hang on a clothes line to dry.

Rough dyeing Sometimes an uneven effect is required; if so, do not soak the material first and do not stir while it is is in the bath. Wring out the cloth instead of squeezing it. Dye colour remover applied unevenly can also be used.

Tie dyeing will give even more tonal variation; the contrast between light and dark areas is much more marked. Tie twists of fabric with string very tightly, either at equally spaced intervals or irregularly according to the effect required, and steep in dye until the right colour is reached. Further

Lining fitches

45° Set Square (helpful for diagonals and right angles)

1"

for stripes and checks.

yardstick

felt pen

measure for mixing dye

tongs for dyeing

dyes

zinc or enamel dye bath

SALT

mexican – stripe cloth with fitches

Syria 6th Century.

free painting.

striping.

Early C19 Kimono.

pointed brush for free painting

The trimmings illustrated opposite are:

a　*Left* two tubular braids through which millinery wire can be threaded (see crowns, p. 114); *right* a lurex and nylon crin braid, for crowns, or for edging frills to make them stand out.

b　A white lace edging for collars, cuffs, necklines etc.; and a black 'lace' braid – the slots would take a cord for extra decoration.

c　A pearl-drop edging which could also be used for crowns; and a narrow embroidered braid for corselets, peasant blouses and petticoats.

d　Two edging braids which can also be used set into seams to emphasize the shape of a bodice or jacket; and another embroidered braid for corselets, etc.

e　Nineteenth-century examples: *left*, a bead, sequin and embroidered motif which could be incorporated in the bodice of a dress or blouse, and *right*, roses which could be cut up as motifs or used in lengths; both have possibilities as hat trimmings.

f　An embroidered strip, useful for dresses, hats or bonnets.

g　A silver edging which, if stiffened, could be used for circlets or crowns or the edges of fairy wings; below it on the right, a bullion braid, now very costly but second-hand pieces can sometimes be found; on the left, a bronze sequin motif for appliqué.

h　A charming braid which, with other braids, could make a Victorian waistband or belt.

Other items not shown, but very necessary for trimming, especially for hats, are artificial flowers and feathers and ribbons. Old ones, when they can be found, are usually the best value. (Instructions for making paper flowers and feathers will be found on p.114.)

tying and dyeing in other colours can be used with very interesting results.

Special effects Dyes can also be splashed on to fabrics or applied broadly with a large brush. They can also be sprayed on; for small areas, a mouth spray may be found adequate, but if a large amount of spraying is to be attempted it is advisable to use some kind of pressure spray such as the aerosol with power unit illustrated on page 105. Dye can also be mixed with methylated spirits (denatured alcohol) for spraying; this is useful if a small quantity of a more intense colour is required, as a more concentrated solution is obtained. It is not wise to treat large areas in this way as the colour tends to rub off. Dye mixed with methylated spirits is an excellent medium to use for dyeing satin or cloth covered shoes.

There is considerable difference in the way that various materials take dye. Natural fibres are the easiest to dye; you will find that certain man-made fibres to not give very satisfactory results, so if in doubt make some tests first. For very pale colours, cold-water dyes may be used, following the instructions on the packet. Helanca tights and leotards take dye very well, but need to be boiled. When dyeing woollen fabrics a little vinegar should be added to the dye bath. Do not boil wool.

Clear up immediately after each dyeing operation to prevent the dye powder speckling the next lot of material. Scour the zinc bath and scrub the stick and tongs thoroughly so that the colour does not come off on any-thing else. Gloves, tights, stockings, etc. can be dyed in a zinc bucket.

PATTERN

Pattern plays an important part in the design of costumes and should be considered from the outset and not added as an afterthought. In certain productions it can be of major importance – especially for stylized plays, ballets and operas, when costumes are often designed around certain motifs. In others, pattern may be used to emphasize character rather than for purely visual effect. The scale of pattern is always very important, and is difficult to teach: it is either an inborn sense or a skill which is slowly acquired by observation and patience. The inexperienced designer is often more likely to make a pattern too small than too large. Border patterns become mean and niggly, motifs are drawn too thinly and tend to look apologetic; on the other hand, boldness can easily deteriorate into clumsi-ness and vulgarity.

It is always better to study original patterns than simply to make them up. Sources for research are almost endless and infinitely varied. Keep a notebook made up of personal sketches of interesting and useful examples, cuttings from newspapers and magazines, and postcards collected from museums and art galleries, to provide a rich fund of reference material. Do not despise the camera as a medium for collecting ideas quickly, especially when travelling abroad.

Always make a good-sized sketch before starting to work so that you have a clear idea at the outset of the final design. Work that has been insufficiently planned usually leads to a waste of both time and materials. Next mark out the design very lightly on the fabric, paying great attention

Natural patterns for adaptation

Tropical Moth

Tropical Butterfly

lower design with felt pen.

C18 Japanese dress.

use a stencil

use a stencil

striping

fabric applique.

thin card.

template for appliqué

Rosettes made from ribbon or crepe paper.

paint or applique

ribbon or coloured tape

103

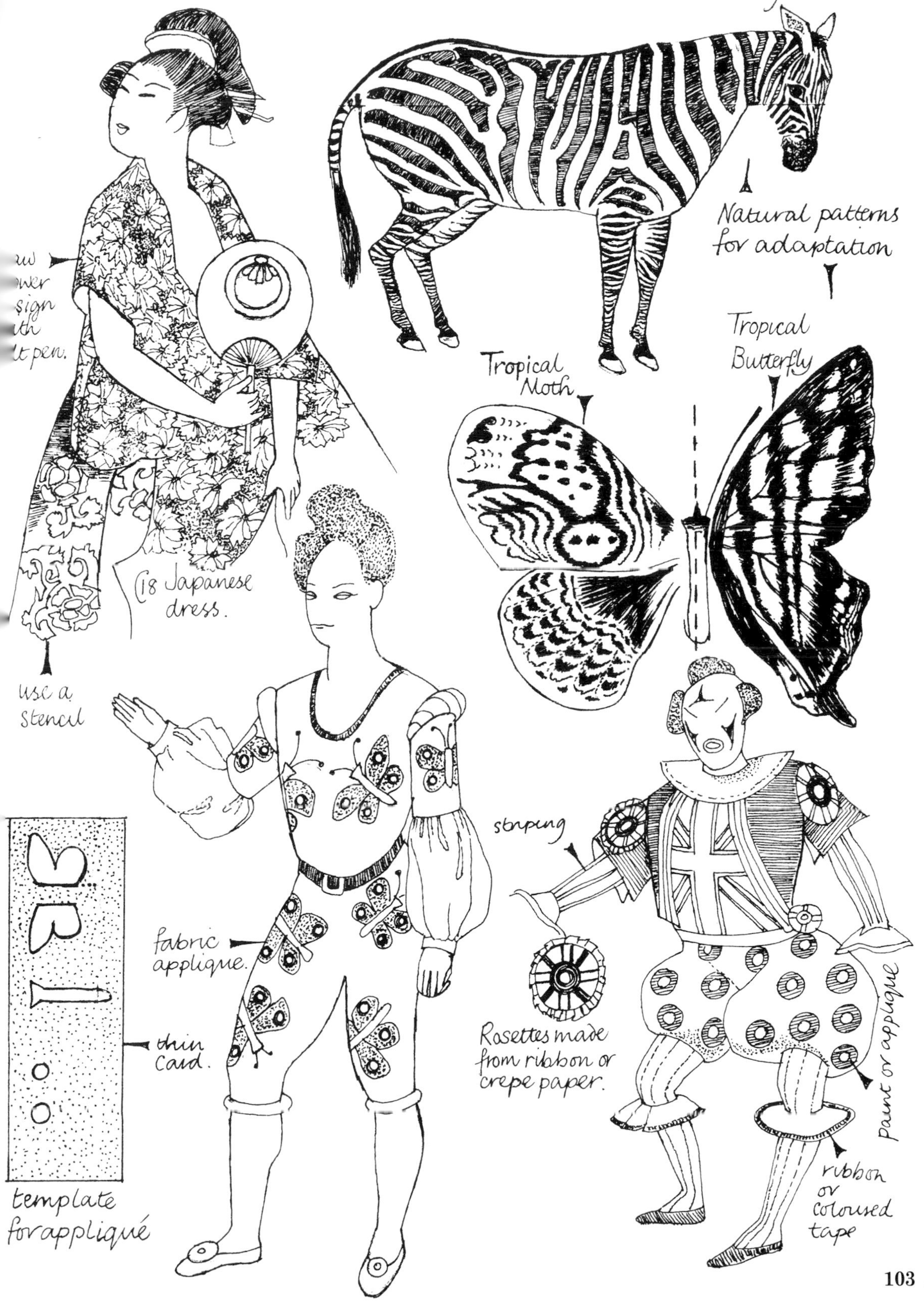

to placing and proportion, then begin work using the sketch as a guide.

There is a fairly large choice of ways in which to apply pattern: it can be painted, printed, or sprayed on the fabric, or it can be glued on, or it can be stitched in place. Often a combination of one or more of these methods is the most satisfactory, as it can add an extra dimension to the design.

There are several different kinds of colours available for use on fabrics. New materials mean that these are constantly changing, so it is advisable to investigate the current market. Most artists' colourmen will stock some varieties and will advise you. Some colours are fixed by the application of a warm iron, such as Flomak Ballpoint Tubes and Pentel Dyeing Pastels; Rowney and Dylon both make a fabric colour which can be fixed by ironing. Felt pens are good for border patterns, but should not be used on garments which are to be washed.

Stencilling For an all-over repeating pattern, a stencil is usually best for at least for some part of the work. Stencil paper is a stiff oiled paper which does not absorb paint; failing this, thin, hard-surfaced card could be used, but this does not stand up to as much wear and the stencil will have to be renewed more frequently. When designing the stencil, remember that there will have to be ties, the bands of paper that hold the pattern together. The design should be bold and simple – any intricate bits will soon tear away or the paint will dribble underneath them. Separate stencils must be cut for different colours.

The piece of material to be printed should be laid on a table covered with several layers of newspaper to give a sympathetic surface on which to work. Draw guide-lines on the material with tailor's chalk to act as a grid for positioning the stencil, but do not necessarily feel cramped by them; a slight variation in the repeat can be very pleasing, but the guide-lines will help to prevent the repeat getting lost altogether or developing a distracting and unwanted slant.

A 1-in lining fitch (a brush with an oblique-angled point) is better than a stencil brush for applying the paint. The thickness of the paint is important: if too thin, it will dribble under the stencil; if too thick it will be difficult to work with and will also stiffen the material so that it no longer drapes or hangs agreeably. Emulsion or acrylic paint tends to have less malleability when dry than fabric colour. With the latter a slight halo tends to spread around the design due to the bleeding of the medium, but this is not usually very noticeable. To thin emulsion paint, use emulsion glaze; to thin acrylic paint, use water; for fabric colour, use tapestry medium or gold size and white spirit (turps substitute). From time to time the stencil must be wiped clean on the underside – always have plenty of cleaning rags handy. See that corks are always replaced in bottles and tops screwed back on to tubes of paint while the work is being carried out; this not only conserves the contents but also guards against spills.

Free brushwork can be combined with stencilling very successfully; it takes away from the rigidity of plain stencilling. When applying pattern to stretchy fabric such as tights and leotards, the garment must be worked on in its stretched condition on a dressmaker's stand.

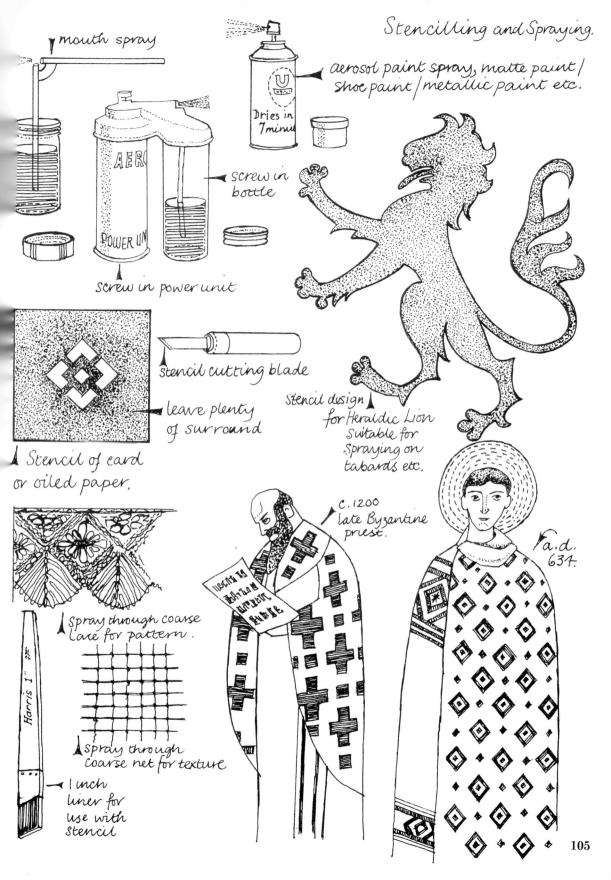

mouth spray

aerosol paint spray, matte paint / shoe paint / metallic paint etc.

Dries in 7 minutes

screw in bottle

AERO

POWER UN

screw in power unit

stencil cutting blade

leave plenty of surround

Stencil of card or oiled paper.

stencil design for Heraldic Lion suitable for spraying on tabards etc.

C. 1200 late Byzantine priest.

a.d. 634.

Spray through coarse lace for pattern.

Harris 1"

Spray through coarse net for texture

1 inch liner for use with stencil

Painting will give a freer result than stencilling, but it needs to be done by a more experienced artist who has confidence and some drawing ability. Simple stencilling can be handed to a careful, neat worker. Fabric colours, designer's colours, emulsion and acrylic paints, or French enamel varnish (which, if unobtainable, can be made from shoe dye, alcohol and shellac) may all be used, mixed to a convenient consistency with the appropriate medium and applied with brushes of various sizes. Brushes may be square-ended or pointed and both hog's bristles and sables will be useful; hog's bristles are good for dry brush work and for stippling. Carefully position the work and sketch in some guide-lines no matter how freely the painting is to be carried out; this ensures that the right proportions are adhered to. Do not use too many colours in one design, or make the painting so important that it is seen only for itself and not as an integral part of the costume. Remember to stand well back from the work from time to time so as to see it in its correct perspective.

Striping Fabric can be striped quite easily with the help of a yardstick or long straight-edge of some kind and a lining fitch. The straight-edge should be held at a slight angle to the work and the brush lightly dragged against it. The brush should not be over-loaded with paint or drips and blobs will be the result. For wider stripes, two lines the requisite distance apart should be drawn and then filled in. Checks and diamonds can be carried out in a similar way. Broad felt pens are excellent for narrow checks and stripes.

Printing Simple fabric printing can be carried out using potato or lino cuts. Potatoes print best with poster colours, which are not washable, but washable fabric printing colours from an artists' colourman will give a permanent result used with lino.

Spraying is a useful way of giving extra life to costumes. It adds a vibrance and interest to the fabric; it can also be used for breaking down clothes when you want them to look old and faded (see page 108). Sometimes, when the pattern of a fabric is a little too bold, some judicious work with the spray gun will help to subdue it. For very small amounts, a mouth spray may be used, otherwise an aerosol with a power unit is useful; there is one on the market for which refills are available, which also has a detachable screw-top jar for the liquid. It is very easy to use, but it is essential to keep it clean or it will soon become clogged and useless. The paint used in these sprays should be rather thin and should be diluted with white spirit (turps substitute). French enamel varnish diluted with methylated spirits (de-natured alcohol) is often better than paint. Another kind of spray to use occasionally is the aerosol sold complete with paint, which may usually be purchased from a well-stocked hardware store. These are especially useful for breaking-down purposes. For spraying silver and gold paint they give a much more even result. Coloured drawing inks are excellent and can be obtained from the manufacturer in large bottles. Although they are not particularly cheap, a little will go quite a long way, and they are particularly easy to handle.

Spraying should not be done in a closed atmosphere, so work near an open window or out of doors; and wear a mask. Be sure there are no naked flames nearby. Release the valve of the spray by exerting very little pressure so that the paint or ink comes out evenly and not in uneven spurts; keep a fairly constant distance from the work and for general spraying keep the spray gently on the move. It is advisable to practise before embarking on a job for the first time. It is nearly always better to do the spraying after the garment is made up, preferably on a dress stand.

A completed costume often gains greatly from a little judicious spraying to take away the rawness from the work and give it a richer tonal quality. A group of costumes sprayed with the same colours gives a great feeling of unity to a production.

Extra textural quality can be achieved by spraying through a wide-mesh material such as coarse net or lace laid lightly on top of the fabric to be sprayed. Spraying may also be combined with painting in pattern work, and can give an added effect to rough dyeing and tie-dyeing. It is also practicable to spray through a stencil but the stencil must be cut with a very wide border of stencil paper around it.

For all work with paints, mix and keep the colours in screw-top jars so that they will not dry up if the work has to be left for a few hours or even a few days. Always wash out brushes after use before the paint dries in them: for fabric colours use turpentine or white spirit, for French enamel varnish use methylated spirits (denatured alcohol), and for emulsion or acrylic paint use cold water. A final wash in hot soapy water is good for the bristles. Paint can be mixed in plastic containers such as cream and yoghurt pots, but guard against leaving the paint in them for too long as sometimes they dissolve, leaving no bottom to the pot and a nasty mess to be cleaned up.

Appliqué is a fairly easy way of carrying out patterns, but it needs careful planning and is usually best in conjunction with some kind of painting and spraying. For gluing fabrics, a latex adhesive such as Copydex or Sobo cannot be improved on, and for braid, beads or for gluing to papier mâché or canvas Bostick or Elmer's glue can be highly recommended. Various textures – thick, thin, rough, shiny – can all be applied to give extra effect; make use of tinsel fabrics and very thick felt. To build up a store of bits and pieces, keep all unwanted scraps of material in a plastic sack. Make full use of things like beads, string, buttons, thick lace, and fabric and straw braids; these can be particularly good for building up chunky, primitive decoration. After gluing them on, they should be sprayed or painted to unify them with the background. Foam rubber, being light, pliable and available in a variety of thicknesses, can often be useful for decoration. It can be used either in strips for border patterns or cut into shapes and applied in conjunction with other materials. Thick industrial felt can also be used like this, but it tends to make the garment very weighty. It is tough to work with and has to be cut with a Stanley (matt) knife. Excellent decorations for breast-plates can be built up in this way. (See also the next chapter.)

The design for appliqué patterns must first be drawn out full size on a piece of paper and a tracing taken from this. The shapes can then be cut from this tracing. If a quantity of similar shapes will be needed, trace the shape onto a piece of firm card and cut a template which can be drawn round with a sharp soft pencil onto the chosen material, moving the template about to get the maximum number of pieces out of the smallest amount of material.

Draw and cut out all the pieces before starting to glue them. If a large number is to be used they can be collected together in shallow box lids and placed conveniently near the work; this makes the actual gluing process very much simpler and quicker, as less time is wasted sorting out the pieces. As with other methods of applying pattern, it is advisable to draw some guide-lines onto the work first.

Trimmings The use of trimmings is fairly obvious, but all too often they can look as though they were an afterthought and have little to do with the original idea. This may be because they are ill-chosen, either too weighty or too light, or of unsuitable or unpleasant texture. Nothing spells death to a costume more quickly than the use of an ill-considered lampshade fringe or one of those characterless furnishing braids which have for so long been synonymous with the theatrical costumier's idea of historical costume. Braid by itself is rarely successful, it often needs the addition of a little paint either brushed or sprayed on. Try to collect samples of the various kinds of fringe and braid which are available and catalogue them in some way; an address book of stockists is also a great time-saver. (See also page 95.)

Note, however, that it is far cheaper to decorate costumes with paint and by applying inexpensive materials than by using many yards of fringe and braid; though this is not necessarily the case when working professionally as the cost of labour for painting jobs has to be borne in mind.

BREAKING DOWN

Old clothes can be broken down for use as costumes for poor characters, tramps, or peasants. Breaking down fabric or garments to just the right state of dilapidation, from slightly shabby to completely ragged, is a great art. A few indiscriminate jabs with the scissors and a blodge of paint will fool no one. Note that clothes wear out at certain points where they rub. Work on the elbows, knees, pockets and button-holes. Ask yourself whether the character dribbles food down the front of his jacket, or has grubby frayed cuffs – or, conversely, whether the clothes should be neatly patched and darned. Should the shoes be scuffed and down at heel, or well-worn but polished?

Useful materials for breaking down are soap, which can be rubbed into collars and cuffs to give the effect of greasiness, machine oil, aerosol paint sprays to give variation of tone, inks, some dyes for stains, and clay or good sticky mud. A circular cheese grater is the best tool for ragging fabrics, with the occasional use of a small hack-saw and some coarse sandpaper.

It is essential to carry out the breaking down process slowly so as to be able to stop at the right moment Recklessness can lead to a handful of shapeless and useless rags. Keep satisfactorily broken-down clothes, they are a valuable asset and can be stored in an old trunk or tea chest in a dry place.

17 · Some simple methods for accessories

For the kind of work described in this section the most useful tools will be: a ruler with a metal edge, for cutting against as well as for measuring; a set square; a Stanley (matt) knife and blades; scissors, large and small; pointed-nose pliers; tweezers; brushes; sewing needles, all sizes; an awl for making holes; a pair of compasses. Bulldog clips in various sizes are very useful for holding work together whilst the glue dries.

It is important, when setting out to decorate costumes and head-dresses and to make costume props, to have a good store of odds and ends of all kinds to draw on. Some likely items are shown on page 112, but there are hundreds of others, both natural and man-made, which could be added. Collect shells, pebbles, corks, conkers, etc. Save remnants of felt, leather and braid – even small scraps can often be used; the shapes left after a design has been cut out can sometimes form the basis for another design. Some ideas are shown (a) for decorating a medieval tunic using lino, screw caps from jars and/or industrial felt – note how the positive and the negative shape of the felt can both be used.

An effective mail surcoat can be made by gluing can lids or foil bottle tops (they need not be identical in size) all over a garment cut in canvas or made up from an old sack (b).

Plastic tubing comes in many thicknesses – with a wire threaded through the centre it can be made to hold all kinds of shapes (c). Paint or spray to finish.

Masks Depending on the number required, masks can be made by the positive or negative method, as shown on page 111. For two or more identical masks it is best to use the negative method using a plaster mould.

First make a working drawing; then take basic measurements – chin to hairline, face width, position of nose etc. – and draft them onto a modelling board (b). Take a lump of clay or plasticine and model the mask on the board (c), keeping the contour sufficiently rounded so that it will fit the face comfortably. Finish the clay smoothly, then cover the surface with petroleum jelly using a brush if there are intricate corners. Tear up newspaper into small pieces, and mix some cold water paste. Cover the clay shape with about six layers of pasted newspaper (d) and allow to dry slowly. Then ease the mask gently away from the clay, using the fingers or a blunt knife (e). Paste another layer of paper onto the inside of the mask and when it is quite dry give it a coat of shellac to harden it. With a sharp blade, cut out spaces for eyes, nose and mouth, making sure they are easy to see and breathe through. The mask can now be painted, with either poster, emulsion or acrylic paints; poster paint will need varnishing when dry.

If more than one mask is needed, a plaster of Paris mould must be made from the clay model. Avoid undercutting on the model, or it will be impossible to pull the mask out of the mould without damaging it. Fix a cardboard wall round the clay model with gummed tape (*f*) to prevent the plaster running away. The plaster must be applied in two layers. Always add plaster to water, not the other way round, or you will have a weak and lumpy plaster. Slowly sieve the powder into a bowl of water, making sure there are no lumps. Let a mound of plaster rise above the water before beginning to mix with the left hand while continuing to sift with the right hand; this must be done rather quickly as the mixture begins to stiffen in a very short time. This operation, though not difficult, may seem a little tricky at first. For the first coat a thin and runny plaster should be used and this is dribbled over the surface of the clay until it is completely covered with no gaps or air bubbles left. Next mix a plaster about the thickness of double cream and coat the mask thickly with this (*g*). Leave the cast to set, then peel away the cardboard wall and take out the clay. Wash the inside of the cast with a brush and soapy water, removing any clay particles which may be lodged in corners. When absolutely dry, grease thoroughly with petroleum jelly making sure every crevice is penetrated. Now line the plaster mould with pasted torn-up newspaper (*h*) in exactly the same way as when making the mask by the positive method. It must be left in the mould until quite dry, after which it can be lifted out and another layer pasted over the greasy surface. When this is dry, sandpaper the mask gently, cut holes for eyes, nose and mouth as before, then paint and varnish. Hair may be added, and eyelets fixed at the side for ties. The mask can be fixed to a stick or trimmed to make a half mask.

The same mould can be used for a latex mask. Do *not* grease the mould, but heat it in a slow oven until hot before filling it with latex solution (obtainable in a can). Leave in a warm place for about ten minutes (experience will teach exactly how long) and then pour the excess latex back into the can. Again leave the mould in a warm place for the latex to dry, then gently ease out the mask, trim with scissors and paint with acrylic colours.

Crowns It is advisable, whenever possible, to use a head block when making crowns to avoid the chance of shrinkage. Guard, too, against overweight; it is surprising how wires and glues add to the weight. A crown which is slightly too big can be adjusted by fixing a small pad of foam rubber inside at the back. Paper patterns should be made to test height and shape as well as size (page 113, *a*). Very simple crowns which will not be used for many performances can be made from pliable card, not too thick or it will crack when bent. For stronger work use buckram. A wire glued and stitched around the base will hold the frame firm, and wire struts fixed in the same way behind the spikes will enable them to be bent to the required shape (*b*). For very heavy-looking crowns, cut the shape in thick industrial felt with a sharp blade and stiffen by painting with shellac almost to saturation point (*c*). The edge is improved if a cord or braid is stitched to it. Once the basic shape is satisfactory, decoration can be glued in place. Wooden domes, diamonds and buttons can be bought cheaply from do-it-yourself stores; shapes can be cut from thick cardboard, or caps from

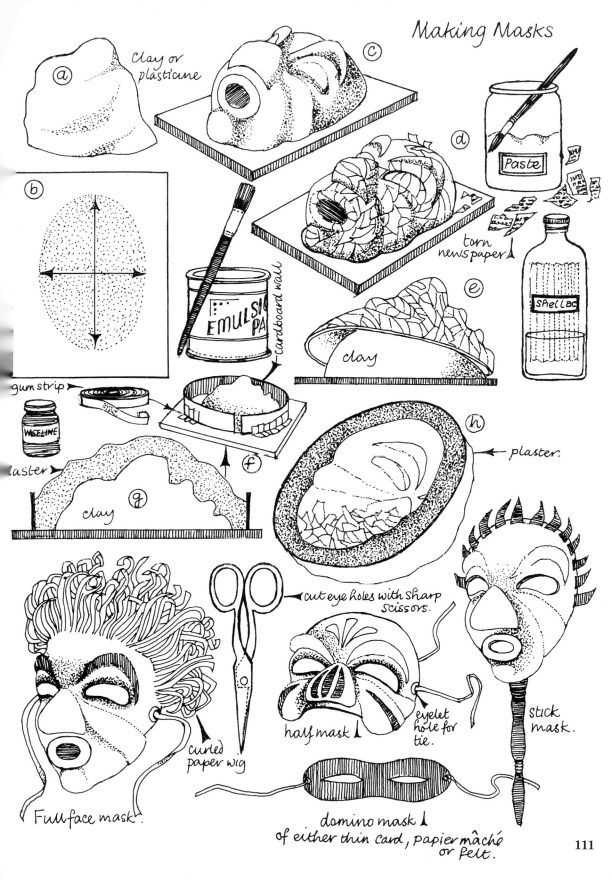

(a) Clay or plasticine

(b)

(c)

(d) Paste

torn newspaper

EMULSION PAINT

cardboard wall

SHELLAC

(e) clay

gum strip

VASELINE

plaster

(f)

(g) clay

(h) plaster

cut eye holes with sharp scissors.

curled paper wig

Full face mask.

half mask

eyelet hole for tie.

stick mask.

domino mask
of either thin card, papier mâché or felt.

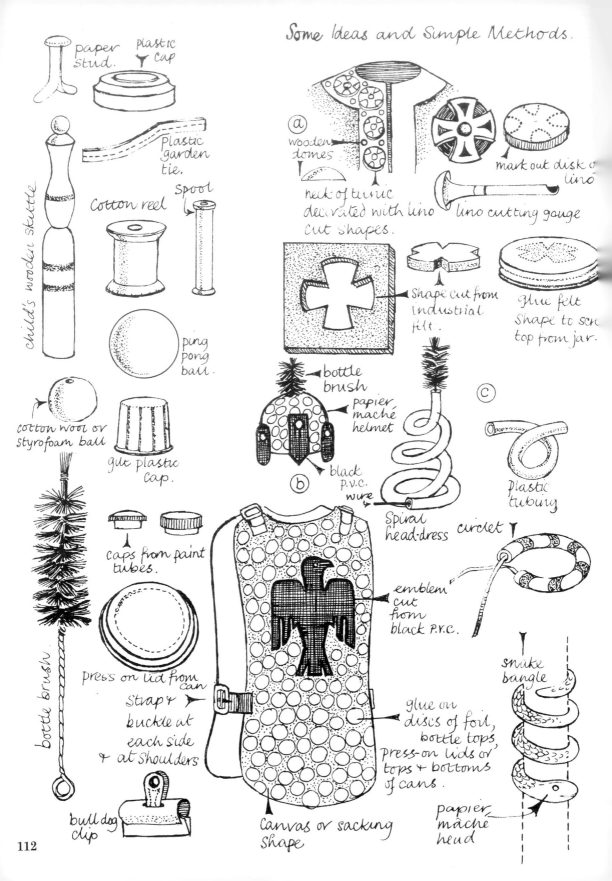

Some Ideas and Simple Methods.

paper stud.

plastic cap

Plastic garden tie.

Cotton reel

Spool

ping pong ball.

child's wooden skittle

cotton wool or styrofoam ball

gut plastic cap.

ⓐ wooden domes

neck of tunic decorated with lino cut shapes.

mark out disk on lino

lino cutting gouge

Shape cut from industrial felt.

glue felt shape to screw top from jar.

bottle brush

papier maché helmet

ⓑ black P.V.C. wire

Spiral head-dress

ⓒ

plastic tubing

circlet

caps from paint tubes.

bottle brush

Press on lid from can

strap & buckle at each side & at shoulders

emblem cut from black P.V.C.

glue on discs of foil, bottle tops, press-on lids or tops & bottoms of cans.

snake bangle

Canvas or sacking Shape

papier maché head

bull dog clip

112

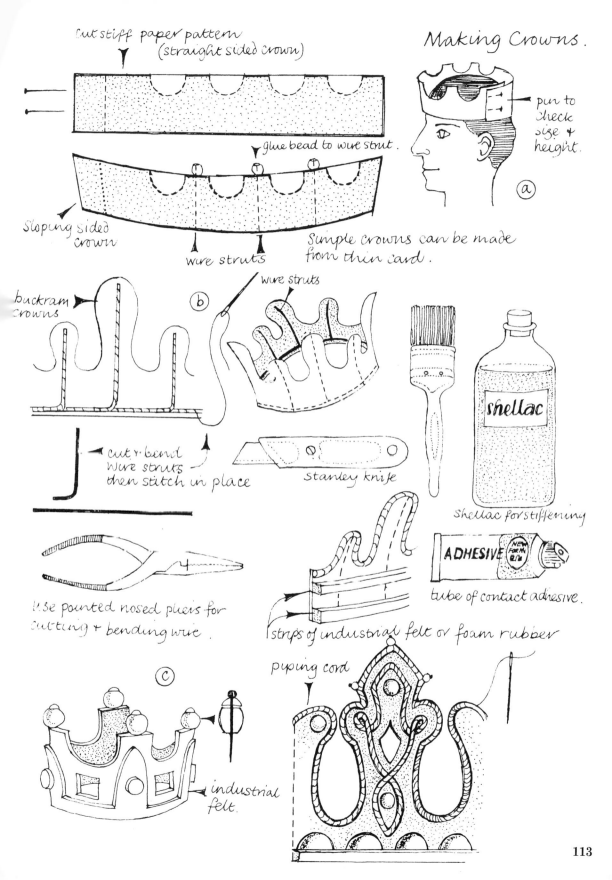

cut stiff paper pattern
(straight sided crown)

Making Crowns.

glue bead to wire strut.

pin to check size & height.

ⓐ

Sloping sided crown

wire struts

Simple crowns can be made from thin card.

buckram crowns

ⓑ

wire struts

cut & bend wire struts then stitch in place

Stanley knife

shellac

Shellac for stiffening

Use pointed nosed pliers for cutting & bending wire.

ADHESIVE NEW FORM 8/16

tube of contact adhesive.

strips of industrial felt or foam rubber

ⓒ

piping cord

industrial felt.

bottles or toothpaste tubes can be very effective. Fix in position with contact adhesive, paint the crown with a coat of shellac and, when this is dry, paint with undercoating – a flat neutral colour is best, such as a dull olive or dead brown. Metallic gold paint can then be brushed on, allowing the undercoat to show through here and there. This gives a three-dimensional effect and avoids the tawdriness of plain gold. Glass jewels can be bought, but too many of these look cheap and amateurish.

For light, fairy-like crowns for dancers, the minimum of buckram and card should be used. A framework of light but firm wire bound with tape is the best foundation (d). Paint this with shellac and then with gold paint, and tie pearl or crystal drops from the loops. If gold or silver tubular braid can be obtained the wire can be pushed through the middle of it and then bent to the required shape (e). Lightweight silver or gold foil-surfaced card or a suitably thick acetate can also be used for the basic shapes (f).

Belts Thick plaited string, sometimes using many strands at once, makes a good basis for belts; leather, plastic and felt may be used with varied textural results. These may be enriched with wooden beads and curtain rings threaded into the plaiting. Trouser hooks make strong and reliable fastenings. Curtain rings can be linked together with leather thonging, using a dab of adhesive at each intersection (g). Blocks of thick lino can be glued to webbing and either engraved with a lino tool or decorated with a jewel surrounded by cord and beads or, much more cheaply, a bottle cap glued on – the various ideas could be combined (h).

Earrings Ear-clips and screws can be bought very cheaply. Glue either a jewel or a cluster of small beads to the clip and add pearls and sequins suspended by nylon thread (i) – tiny dabs of contact adhesive applied with a toothpick will ensure that the beads do not fall off.

Feathers and flowers Making feathers from tissue or crêpe paper is extremely simple and effective and also very cheap. If crêpe paper is used, the grain of the paper should run across the feather. Cut the feather from several thicknesses of paper and make two lines of stitching up the middle to form a channel into which you insert a piece of galvanized wire (page 117). Cut the fronds and draw them across the blunt edge of a dinner knife while the paper is held under slight tension by the thumb. Finally bend the central wire into shape. For variegated colour spray lightly with ink or paint.

Flowers are best made in tissue paper as this gives a lighter and more delicate touch than the coarser texture of crêpe paper. First take a length of wire and bend it into a loop at the top, as shown. Cut a piece of paper and fringe the ends, and thread this through the loop to form the stamens. Then cut about half a dozen paper circles, varying in size and tone or colour, for the petals. Smear a small dab of adhesive in the centre of each one and thread them onto the wire, pinching the centre to the depth of about half an inch; this will give the petals interesting pleats and frills. Cut a length of green paper for the stem and bind it round the wire, starting at the bottom and using a little glue to keep the binding in place. Add the calyx and the flower is finished. Leaves can be cut from paper, felt or leather or

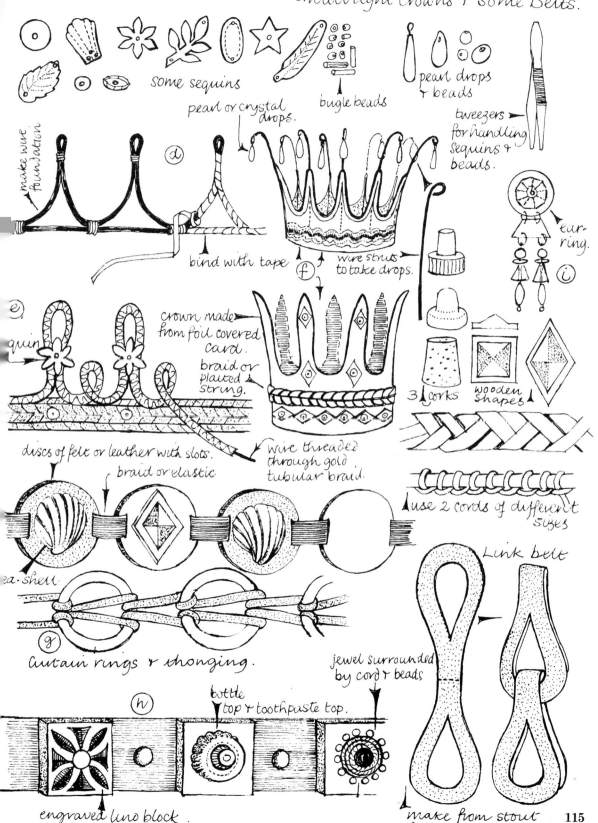

some sequins

pearl or crystal drops.

bugle beads

pearl drops & beads

tweezers for handling sequins & beads.

make wire foundation

(a)

bind with tape

(f)

wire struts to take drops.

ear-ring.

(i)

(e)

sequin

crown made from foil covered card.

braid or plaited string.

3 corks

wooden shapes

discs of felt or leather with slots.

braid or elastic

wire threaded through gold tubular braid.

use 2 cords of different sizes

Link belt

sea-shell

jewel surrounded by cord & beads

(g)

Curtain rings & thonging.

(h)

bottle top & toothpaste top.

engraved lino block.

make from stout felt or leather.

115

from muslin or organdie for more delicate results; wire veins are glued down the centre so that the leaves can be bent and twisted and then wired to the stem. Similar leaves can be attached to a wire frame to make a garland for the head. This could be sprayed gold. Cheap fabric and plastic flowers are an alternative, but they are usually not very pleasing and need some work on them to make them acceptable.

Beads A variety of differently shaped beads can be made by winding long strips of newspaper pasted with cold water paste round a greased knitting needle; when dry they will slip off the needle and can be painted and varnished and used in a number of ways – on crowns, belts, earrings, necklaces, etc.

In the us there is a sculpting material called Celastic which can be used in a similar way to papier mâché for making costume props and accessories.

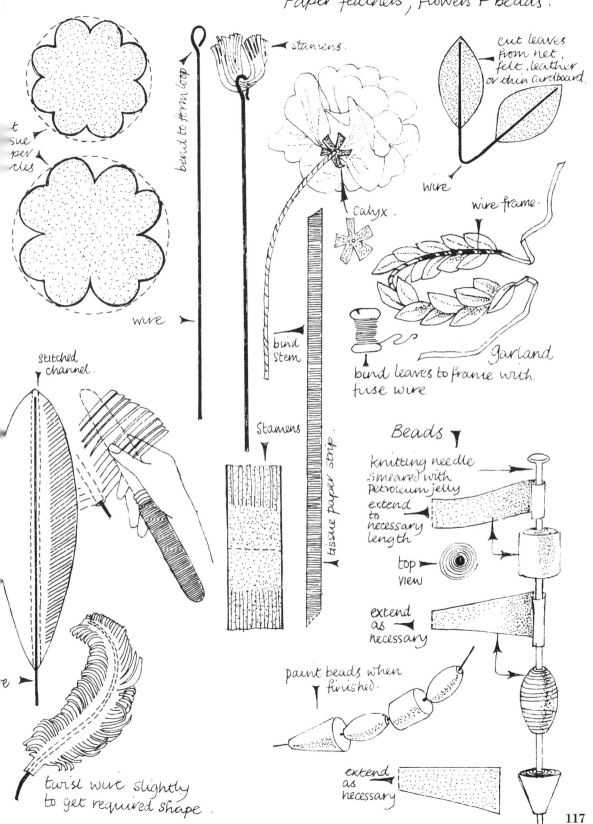

Paper feathers, flowers & beads.

tissue paper circles

bend to form loop

stamens.

cut leaves from net, felt, leather or thin cardboard

wire

wire frame.

calyx.

wire

bind stem

tissue paper strip

bind leaves to frame with fuse wire

Garland

stitched channel.

wire

Stamens

twist wire slightly to get required shape.

Beads

knitting needle smeared with petroleum jelly extend to necessary length

top view

extend as necessary

paint beads when finished.

extend as necessary

117

18 · Musicals and pantomimes

Some types of costumes which occur frequently in musicals are shown on pages 119 and 121. Boldly patterned shirts, neckerchiefs, jeans, bib-and-brace dungarees make a useful start. Stout belts, smart braided waistcoats, strong boots and wide-brimmed hats in felt or straw help to build up the Western style. The Indian costume is contrived from a blanket boldly appliquéd, with a cloth fringe stitched around the edge. A fringed tunic of imitation suede cloth can be decorated with wooden beads.

Calf-length print cotton dresses, with plenty of crisp petticoats, look charming on dancers. Be sure to have plenty of fullness in the skirts (see page 132 for skirt patterns). Braid, ribbons or, more cheaply, strips of fabric can be used to outline flounces and frills and to trim bodices. Dresses for dancers should not be cluttered with too many trimmings or the line of movement will be confused. Straw hats, bonnets or nineteenth-century cotton sun bonnets are pretty, youthful and becoming. Older women can have similar, floor-length dresses with triangular shawls or short capes.

The next page of drawings shows an eastern dancer (*a*), using the trouser pattern on page 125 and fixing the top of the trousers to elasticated bikini briefs; the collar pattern is given on page 121. Bikini briefs can be used as a foundation for many kinds of skirt, holding the garment firmly in place in spite of vigorous movement; folds and pleats are more easily controlled in this way – see the draped loincloth (*c*), useful for eastern slaves. Plastic raffia, which comes in an excellent range of colours, makes an attractive Hawaiian skirt (*d*). Sailor costumes can be built up from navy blue flared trousers and tight sweaters (or, alternatively, white for tropical wear) with the addition of a sailor collar (pattern, page 125).

Singlets (undershirts) or tank tops can be dyed, painted, appliquéd, etc; boy dancers will appreciate the amount of freedom they give (*e*).

Eliza Doolittle (*f*), Shaw's flower girl given a rebirth in the musical *My Fair Lady*, wears a costume adaptable to any similar character – a sensible wool shawl, serviceable apron and boots, together with a cheerful check blouse and a hat gaudily trimmed with feathers and artificial flowers. The final page in this section gives a kimono pattern (bearing in mind the Gilbert and Sullivan comic opera, *The Mikado*). Two alternative sleeves are shown – in both cases they are stitched to the armhole only along the line of dots, leaving the characteristic under-arm gap of approximately 6in for freer movement. The sash, a straight piece of fabric called an *obi*, should be lined with stiff canvas. The facing, which stands up round the back of the neck and extends about half way down the fronts, is a straight folded strip, often matching the lining of the kimono.

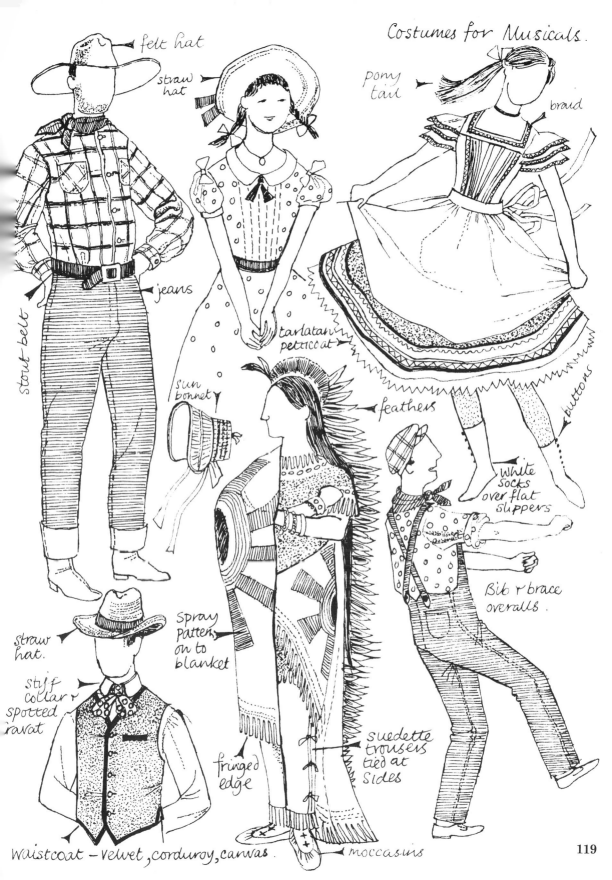

Costumes for Musicals.

felt hat

straw hat

pony tail

braid

jeans

stout belt

tarlatan petticoat

buttons

sun bonnet

feathers

white socks over flat slippers

Bib & brace overalls.

spray pattern on to blanket

straw hat.

stiff collar & spotted cravat

fringed edge

suedette trousers tied at sides

moccasins

Waistcoat – Velvet, corduroy, canvas.

119

Costumes for Musicals

circular or semi-circular collar

black straw hat trimmed with paper flowers + feathers

d

strands of plastic raffia, looped & tied

fringed woollen shawl

a

transparent eastern trousers over bikini briefs

sacking apron

Eliza Dolittle (London flower girl)

f

e

c

loin cloth draped over bikini briefs

b

Bright coloured tank tops + jersey trousers allow dancers to move easily.

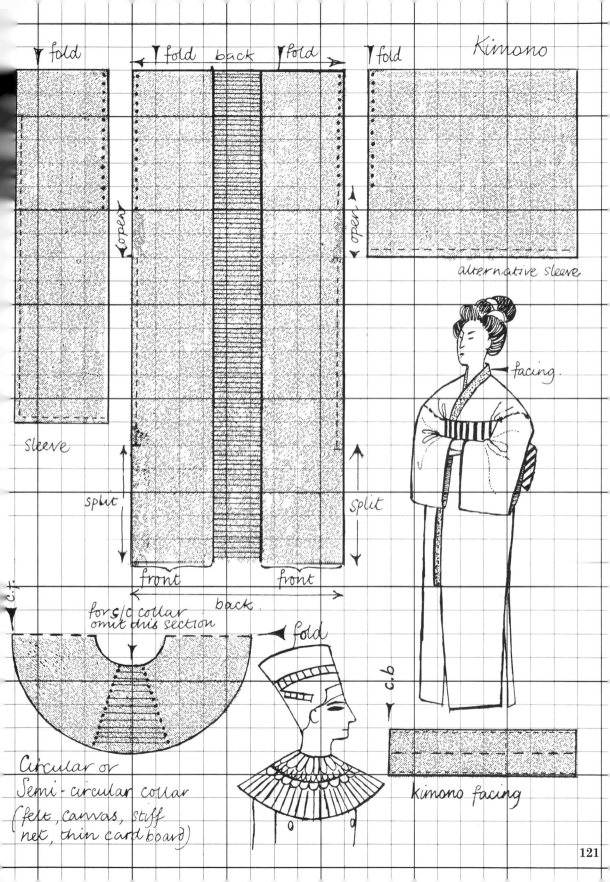

fold   fold   back   fold   fold   Kimono

open   open

alternative sleeve

facing.

sleeve

split   split

front   front

c.f.

back

for S/C collar
omit this section

fold

c.b

Circular or
Semi-circular collar
(felt, canvas, stiff
net, thin card board)

kimono facing

121

In England, winter usually brings a rush of theatrical activity with entertainments planned for the Christmas season and New Year, a number of them light-hearted, with dancing and music, for the whole family to visit. Comical animals, both two- and four-legged, are often included as well as clowns and slapstick funny men with bags of flour, bowls of custard and pails of wallpaper paste. Some of these characters are part of the pantomime tradition with its hilarious, topsy-turvey world where principal boys are played by glamorous girls and dames and ugly sisters by male comedians. Opposite, Cinderella is shown in her ragged skirt, sweeping the kitchen (a). Old costumes can be broken down into rags as described on page 108. The Ugly Sister (c), usually played by a man, is a larger-than-life character and should be dressed with exaggeration. Most pantomimes include an undressing scene for the Dame which gives scope for all kinds of undergarments such as the pantalettes made from flags (d), the knickers with appliquéd hearts (e) and the chemise decorated with iron-on letters (f). Do not be afraid to use clear, bright colours to give impact to the comedian's clothes.

The diagram (g) shows a felt over-shoe (see also page 135) which can be worn over sneakers to imitate the big flat fleet often seen on clowns. Cut the sole in strong industrial felt; the upper part should be less thick. Stitch a tape loop at the heel and slot a length of tape through the front. Cross the ends, thread through the loop at the back and tie round the ankle.

Animals come into all kinds of entertainments and are always a great success. A dragon costume (page 124) can be made from painted hessian (burlap) with raffia inserted into the back seam and knotted into spikes. A piece of cane round the middle holds out the shape (see diagram) – the tape across the wearer's back keeps the cane bent and holds the arch away from the wearer's body. The two-man horse should also be made from hessian or scene painters' canvas. The heads, in both cases, can be made from papier mâché (see masks and balloon heads).

For Puss-in-Boots use an all-over garment (pattern on page 125). Jersey fabric can be painted, but if fur fabric is used it must be sprayed through a stencil to prevent the pile from clotting.

Some Pantomime Costumes.

Cinderella - simple peasant blouse ⓐ

it — ...yers of ...gged with ...ese ...ter

Ugly Sister or Pantomime Dame

black net mittens

Aladdin (Finale Costume)

cane

ⓒ

whole socks over sneakers

pantalettes made from flags ⓓ

slot for elastic

ⓔ

red plastic nose

ⓑ cheese grater for ragging fabrics

cane

felt or suedette tunic with epaulette

ⓖ

Brokers Man (funny man)

Robin Hood

ⓕ

LOVE ME

chemise 123

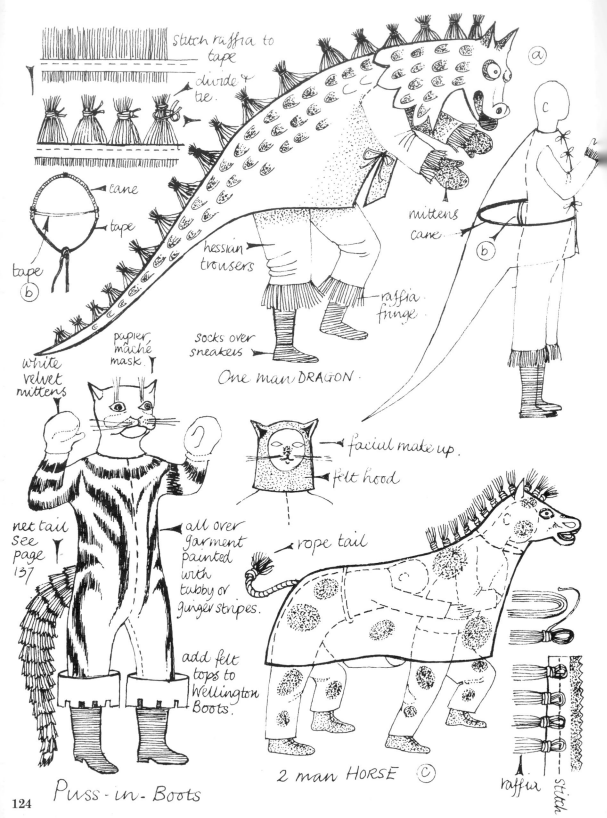

stitch raffia to tape

divide & tie.

cane

tape

tape

ⓑ

white velvet mittens

papier mâché mask

ⓐ

mittens cane

ⓑ

hessian trousers

raffia fringe

socks over sneakers

One man DRAGON

facial make up.

felt hood

rope tail

net tail see page 137

all over garment painted with tabby or ginger stripes.

add felt tops to Wellington Boots.

2 man HORSE ⓒ

Puss-in-Boots

raffia

stitch

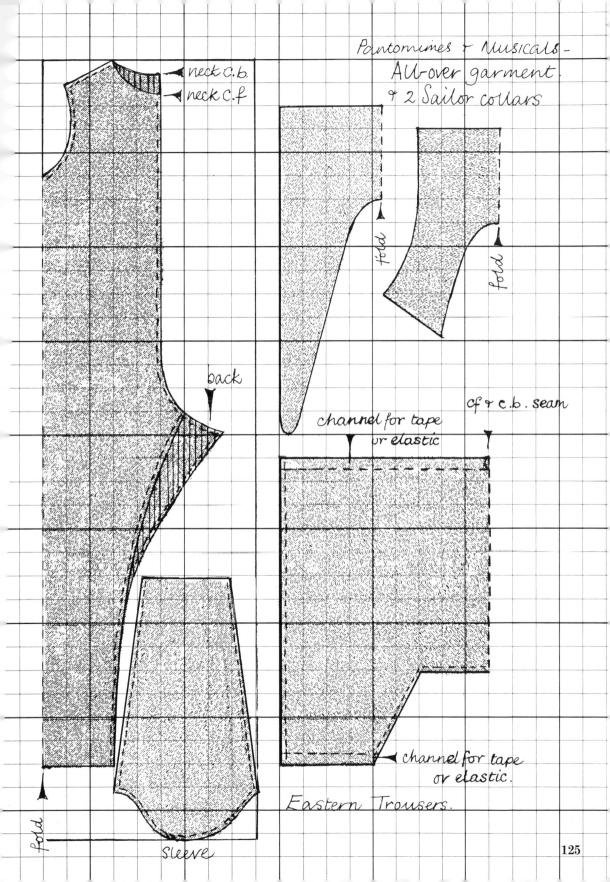

neck c.b.

neck c.f

fold

fold

back

cf & c.b. seam

channel for tape or elastic

channel for tape or elastic.

Eastern Trousers.

fold

sleeve

125

19 · Pageants and carnivals

Pageants are usually performed in celebration of events of local or historical significance. People of the neighbourhood, many of whom are not normally involved in theatrical performances, foregather to enjoy a communal activity. The roles may not be individually demanding, but as pageants frequently involve large numbers the organization must be well-prepared and the costumes should be of the kind that can easily be achieved. Many of the ideas in this book can be applied to pageants and may be adapted to very simple principles involving garments which can be found in most people's wardrobes. Ingenuity is the keynote of this kind of costume design.

A quantity of skirts of various shapes and sizes is a useful nucleus for the women's costumes. Sometimes it is possible to obtain a bale of cloth cheaply through a local manufacturer, otherwise a collection of unwanted sheets, curtains and bedspreads can be made up into skirts and then dyed to suitable colours. Some diagrams for different skirt shapes are shown on page 132. For gathered skirts (*a* and *b*) any number of widths of fabric can be used according to the fullness required. Skirt *a* can be used over hip pads, stiff petticoats or the early crinoline; in movement it spins out to a bell shape. The gathers round the waist may be rather bulky, especially if a thick fabric is used. It makes a good peasant skirt. By substituting gores for straight panels (*b*), the amount of bulk around the waist is reduced while retaining the same width at the hem. When spun round, this skirt takes an A-line. It can be worn over an Elizabethan hoop or is suitable for the later crinoline from 1850 onwards.

Skirts *c* and *d* are suitable for dancers. Both will spin out as shown in the drawings; the gathered circular skirt is especially good for very lightweight fabrics such as georgette or chiffon. The hem should be rolled or bound, or even left raw, as a heavy hem will hamper both the hang of the skirt and the movement.

Stitch skirts to a petersham (grosgrain) band; a trouser hook makes a strong fastening. For peasants or rough characters, they can have a tape or elastic run through a slot at the top so that they will fit different waist measurements without alteration.

Pyjama trousers, particularly the striped variety, are excellent for a multitude of characters; they too will fit different waist sizes and are usually of a fabric which dyes well. Sets of trousers can also be made up cheaply from a pyjama pattern. Some stores conveniently sell pyjama trousers separately from the jackets. These trousers can be tied round the legs with thongs or cross gartered, or tucked into boots to form breeches. Track suit trousers also make excellent breeches. Ski pants can have a strip of coloured plastic adhesive tape fastened down the side to make

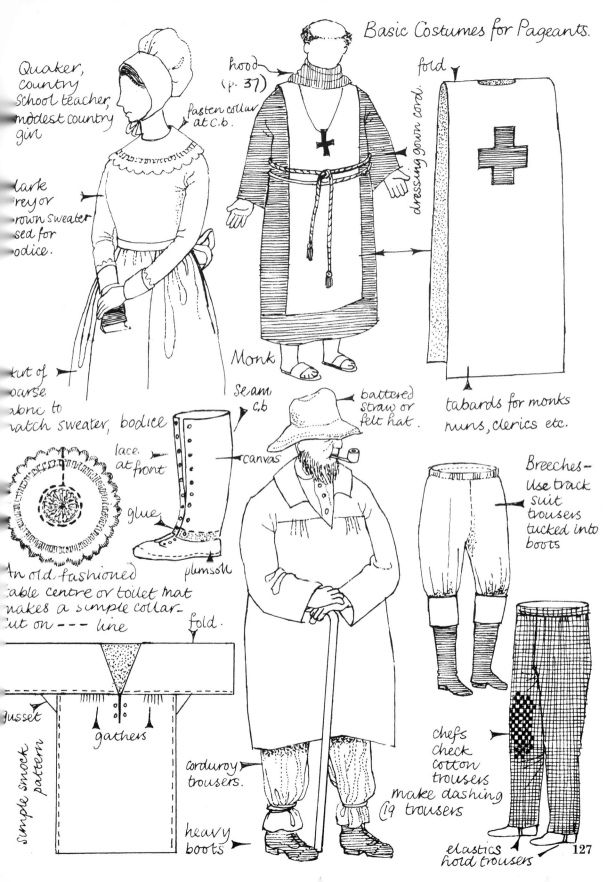

Quaker, country school teacher, modest country girl

fasten collar at c.b.

dark grey or brown sweater used for bodice.

skirt of coarse fabric to match sweater, bodice

hood (p. 37)

Monk

dressing gown cord.

fold

tabards for monks nuns, clerics etc.

An old fashioned table centre or toilet mat makes a simple collar - cut on --- line

seam c.b.

lace at front

glue

canvas

plimsoll

battered straw or felt hat.

Breeches - Use track suit trousers tucked into boots

simple smock pattern

gusset

fold.

gathers

corduroy trousers.

heavy boots

chefs check cotton trousers make dashing C19 trousers

elastics hold trousers

127

military trousers. The checked cotton trousers used by chefs are cheap and adaptable. Corduroy trousers can be used for country characters such as the yokel in the smock on page 127. Any trousers which are no longer wanted can be cut off below the knee and stitched into a band or elasticated to make a very acceptable pair of breeches.

Bath towels of various sizes, which are often available in lovely colours nowadays, have a number of uses: small towels make turbans, larger ones fastened together at the shoulders make tunics, and really large bath sheets make cloaks. Towelling hangs and drapes well and also takes dye satisfactorily. Torn-up towels make very effective rags.

For both men and women, the other really indispensable garment is the sweater. Various weights are suitable for different purposes. For women, they can be worn with collars and shawls, boleros and jackets, etc.; for men they can be adapted with collars and cravats, and waistcoats and capes can be worn over them. Sleeveless tunics and dresses such as the extremely basic robe or tunic shown opposite make excellent over-garments. These can be made from cheap tubular jersey or seamed at the sides; any available fabric can be used up in this way. A number of these in varied lengths and good colours will prove a great asset when equipping crowds.

In these days of fashion shoes, providing suitable footwear for one or two hundred people can be quite a problem. The first principle to bear in mind is that whereas it is possible to disregard dark-coloured shoes the eye is always drawn to anything light-coloured on the feet, especially in a group of people. For early periods, persuade all performers to bring their own sneakers and large, thick neutral-coloured socks to wear over them. Black socks over sneakers will also look like elastic-sided boots. Simple leather or rubber boots are often useful, and baseball boots can be sprayed or painted brown or black. A way of making boots from sneakers is shown on page 127. Gaiters, spats and sandals are useful. Early shoes for Greek, Roman, primitive or early medieval characters can be made from ovals of thick felt, leather or canvas with holes punched round the edge and a leather thong threaded through and tied, as shown opposite.

Heads should be covered whenever possible to save the expense and bother of hiring wigs. Collect all kinds of unwanted felt and straw hats which can be adapted to the special requirements of the pageant. Simple caps, headscarves, wimples and bonnets for women, and bag hats, felt and straw pull-on hats for men, should be used as much as possible. Women's hats with wide brims can be altered to make broad-brimmed seventeenth-century hats or curled eighteenth-century tricornes for men. Top hats and bowler hats can sometimes be borrowed.

The truly effective pageant usually depends on good masses and groupings with just a few spectacular characters, so it is essential to think in terms of massed colours which look good together and of simplicity and unity within groups, plus the occasional detailed and special costume for an important character.

Make sure that performers remove spectacles and unsuitable jewelry, as these can provide an anachronistic and jarring note.

turban, eastern or medi·eval small towel.

epskin ur rug.

sacking tunic

fur rug

cover swim trunks with fur or sacking

bath towels

blanket or travelling rug.

thick sweater

Pyjama trousers

Simple robe for man or woman, with draw-string at waist + neck–use old curtains, sheets or sacking.

Costumes for a street carnival should contribute to the mood of merriment and jollification. Colours need to be bright, even garish, and the conception can be bizarre and inconsequential, creating a zany world outside the normal hum-drum of the everyday street.

Because of this it is a good idea to play about with shapes and sizes and to invent characters with giant heads, fat figures, elongated figures and figures which tower above the others in a procession. Costumes with glitter and movement to them are also effective; ribbons and streamers will be caught by the breeze and balloons will bob about, and costumes with bells will jingle as the wearer moves.

As most carnivals take place on one day only the outlay on materials should be kept to a minimum and the decoration should rely on bold rather than detailed work. Immediate impact is an important factor, for the procession passes quickly and spectators must receive an instant impression.

For the giant-headed figure (d) use a strong paper sack for the foundation. Open it out so that it will comfortably accommodate the head and shoulders, and then paste several layers of newspaper onto it with cold-water paste and allow to dry. It should now be quite firm and any other features such as the horns shown in the illustration, nose and ears can be added. Give the head an all-over coat of emulsion paint with a broad brush. When quite dry, detail and pattern can be added and a large mouth cut out with a sharp blade at a convenient place for the wearer to look through. The eyes are discs of foil-covered card attached with cloth strips or ribbon so that they will move when the figure is in action, giving liveliness to the character. Fix strips of brightly-coloured cloth or crêpe paper to the bottom of the mask and the tops of the rubber boots – they would be effective round the armholes as well. The tail is made of plastic tubing bound with paper with a tuft at the end of crêpe paper or feathers, and is tied to a waist belt.

The tall figure (c) is constructed on a long pole which passes through a large ball (the head) and finishes with a small ball fixed on top, as shown in the drawing. The hoops (children's hoops, cane, spring curtain wire or whalebone) are not absolutely essential but they will help to make the shape more easily manoeuvrable and make it easier for the wearer to see through the netted holes. The decoration and trimming should be light-hearted. This costume is worn over a long skirt or patterned trousers.

Finally, a hobby horse (a) for a gallant knight or lady to ride! Cut the head from plywood with a fret or jigsaw. Slot it into a short length of 2-in diameter dowel; then fit a 1-in diameter broomstick into a hole drilled in the other end of the dowel (see diagram b). Insert a hand rod through the head where shown. Paint, then trim with shiny paper and braid.

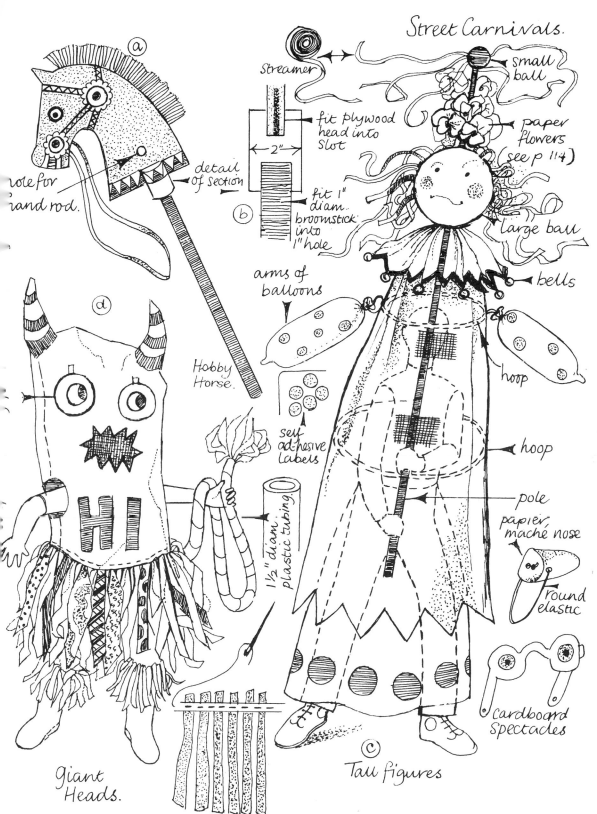

Street Carnivals.

(a)

hole for hand rod.

detail of section

(b)

streamer

small ball

paper flowers (see p 114)

fit plywood head into slot

2"

fit 1" diam broomstick into 1" hole

large ball

bells

arms of balloons

Hobby Horse.

hoop

hoop

self adhesive labels

pole

papier mache nose

round elastic

1½" diam plastic tubing

cardboard spectacles

(d)

HI

Giant Heads.

(c)

Tall figures

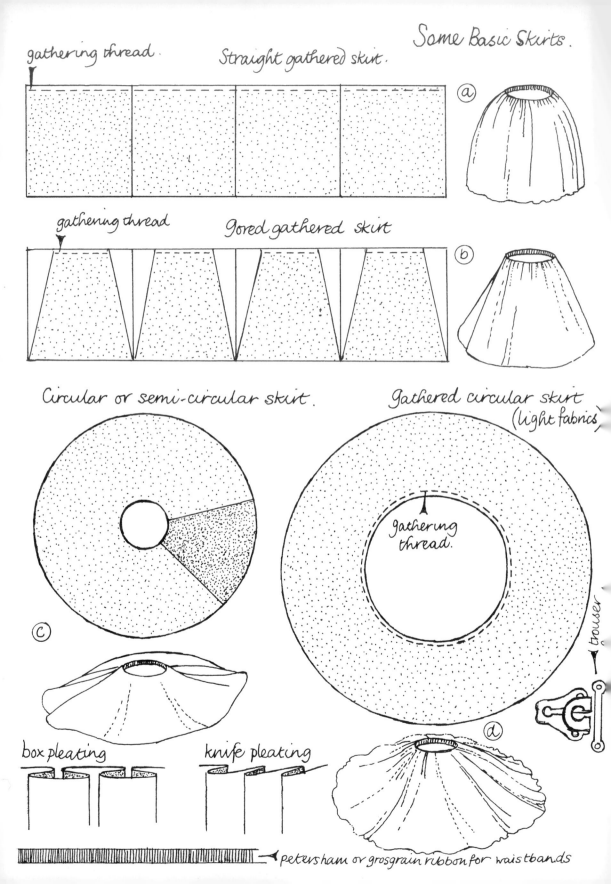

Some Basic Skirts.

Straight gathered skirt.

gathering thread.

ⓐ

Gored gathered skirt

gathering thread

ⓑ

Circular or semi-circular skirt.

ⓒ

Gathered circular skirt (light fabrics)

gathering thread.

ⓓ

trouser

box pleating

knife pleating

petersham or grosgrain ribbon for waistbands

20 · Especially for schools

Costumes for school plays must necessarily be of a simple nature, and it is better so, for too elaborate a costume can very easily swamp a child's performance. The costumes should encourage and emphasize the enthusiastic liveliness of young actors and be fun to wear. They should be designed and planned so that they can be quickly and easily made by parents, teachers or senior pupils while involving younger ones in many of the ideas and simpler operations.

The paper sack costumes shown on page 135 can be made by all but the very youngest children. Obtain some of the strong paper sacks now on the market, use the sealed bottom of the sack for the shoulders and cut a hole for the head, and make two holes in the sides for the arms. The sacks can then be painted to represent any character, such as the clown or the tortoise shown in the drawings. Use large brushes to paint the areas of background colour and smaller brushes to sharpen up the design with detail. The sacks can be teamed up with other items which may be found in the child's wardrobe, such as striped socks and sweaters or leotards. The idea for the tortoise shows boots and mittens made from foam rubber stitched together with a large packing needle and carpet thread, or glued with a suitable cement round the edges. The boots can be sprayed or painted, or they can be bound with strips of cloth to give the wrinkled and creased effect necessary for a tortoise. The war dance costume uses half a paper sack strengthened at the waist with a strip of canvas from which cork balls or conkers are suspended (these could first be dipped in paint).

Very simple but effective masks can be made from strong paper bags, or from bags made of strong coloured paper easily stitched together at the sides with a sewing machine. Cut paper shapes may be pasted onto the bags, or they can be painted with bold patterns. For beards and hair, fringe paper with scissors and curl the fronds against the back of a dinner knife (see feathers, page 117). Put the bag on the head and mark the position of the eye holes and an air hole for breathing through. Masks are much more effective and dramatic if the proportions are quite different from those of the actual head, so exaggerate height and breadth and the placing and size of the features. The paper bag can be worn with the seams at the side or at the back and front; the latter gives a firmer result if a beak or large nose is to be added. Both sacks and paper bags will last for several performances if made of good strong paper, and accidental rips can be mended by pasting a paper patch on the inside.

Another kind of mask can be made from a stocking pulled over the head. Mark out the position of the eyes, nose and mouth, smear a contact adhesive on the area which is to be cut away, and allow to dry before using the scissors; this will prevent the threads from running. The leg and foot of the stocking can be tightly twisted and stitched to make a decorative top-knot or a pig-tail (see drawings of clown and Chinaman).

Plain T-shirts lend themselves to being painted or, even easier, can be drawn on with broad-tipped felt pens which have the great advantage of not stiffening the fabric. (Be sure to keep the tops on the pens when not in use to prevent them drying out.) Leotards and tights can also be treated in this way. Remember, though, that felt pens will wash out.

Still using paper, but this time in scraps, page 136 shows a way of making grotesque carnival heads based on balloons. Inflate the balloon to the required size and grease it all over with petroleum jelly. Then paste strips and pieces of newspaper over the entire area to a depth of about five layers, using cold water paste. Leave this to dry in a warm (not hot) atmosphere; if the drying process is too sudden or the place too warm the air inside the balloon will expand and crack open the papier mâché casing. When quite dry, slowly let out the air. The papier mâché shape *may* crumple slightly, but this should not cause too much alarm. The deflated balloon can be removed from the paper shape which can then be re-inflated by blowing into the open end. For painting the papier mâché, French enamel is best because, being spirit-based, it does not soften the paper. Hats and head-dresses such as the turban on page 38 can be made in the same way, gluing the finished shape to a felt cap (*a*). These carnival heads and head-dresses are very light to wear. It may be advisable to fix the heads to a shoulder harness (see page 137) to prevent them slipping about.

The turban head-dress would look well for an Eastern King in a nativity play and could be worn with a costume like the one on page 137. Make a simple coat, cut as shown in the diagram and fastened at the front with ties. Patchwork is a useful way of using up scraps left over from dressmaking and when used judiciously the effect can be quite rich and certainly most effective. Real patchwork would be very time-consuming, but if the coat is made from an unwanted sheet, table cloth or curtain the various patchwork pieces can be pinned to fit this base and stitched on with a zig-zag machine stitch – in this way the garment will have a built-in lining. The patchwork can be of a random higgledy-piggledy nature, or, if you have a large choice of pieces, it can be planned in a more controlled scheme using a limited colour or pattern range. Patchwork garments used in conjunction with other items of clothing is another possibility and could be used as a theme for certain kinds of production.

Page 137 also shows ways of dealing with wings (another idea can be seen on page 38 in the drawing of the Ethiopian angel). The frames for the fairy's wings are made from galvanized wire bent and bound with either fuse wire or carpet thread as indicated; smear the thread with contact adhesive to fix it in position, paying particular attention to the knots. Then smear the frames with the same glue and lay either net or organdie on top, allow to dry, and finally trim the fabric to shape with sharp scissors. Another excellent and easy way to cover the frame is to use plastic cling wrap (normally used for food and bought by the roll). It can be cut roughly to shape, slightly larger than the frame, then laid on and folded over the wire so that it clings to itself. Decorate wings with sequins and puffs of metallic spray paint or small scraps of foil. Stitch the wings to a harness as shown, and leave an opening in the back of the costume to accommodate

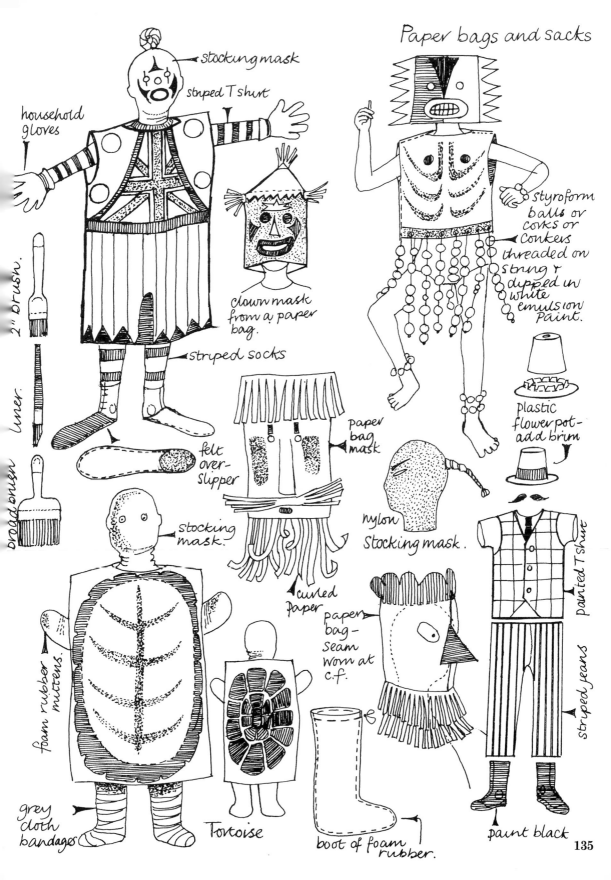

stocking mask

striped T shirt

household gloves

styroform balls or corks or conkers threaded on string & dipped in white emulsion paint.

clown mask from a paper bag.

striped socks

felt over-slipper

paper bag mask

plastic flower pot - add brim

2" brush.

liner.

broad onion

stocking mask.

curled paper

nylon stocking mask.

painted T shirt

paper bag - seam worn at c.f.

striped jeans

foam rubber mittens.

grey cloth bandages

Tortoise

boot of foam rubber.

paint black

135

inflate balloon to required size

smear all over with vaseline (petroleum jelly)

torn newspaper.

flour and water paste

Let out air. slowly

cone of paper

household rubber glove

secure at wrist with elastic band

toe nails from foil

cut up plastic cartons to make claws.

TIGER

Tiger

cut into tabs - bend inwards & upwards - glue to cap

paint or decorate (eg. as turban)

paint white - glue foil chips all over head.

@

stitch to form cap

1/4" turning

1/4 of head circumference cut 4.

Clown head.

polystyrene drinking cup.

strips of clear plastic threaded into coarse net

Ghost

white socks or tights

136

Wings, Tails & Patches.

galvanised wire

bend wire to form frame

simple wire frame

bind wires with tape.

stitch wires to base.

ear-ring

thread

net frill

use big bright umbrella

head-dress based on balloon

felt beard

cover wire frame with cling wrap.

ties.

stitch at c.b.

use a broad tip felt pen

glue sequins with contact adhesive.

velvet facing.

Eastern King - Nativity Play.

Spray a puff of metallic paint.

7 mins

sequins.

137

them. Butterfly wings can be made from a floating fabric such as rayon georgette (net is too stiff) stitched to the costume at one side of the back opening only, so that it is possible to get in and out of the costume, and fastened to the wrists with elastic. When using a felt pen on thin fabrics such as georgette, it is advisable to stretch the fabric onto a flat surface with drawing pins to keep it rigid. Apart from drawing veins and shapes, a dotting technique is the best way of filling in an area with colour. When gluing sequins onto fabrics, use a transparent contact adhesive, applying it *sparingly* with a sharpened matchstick or a toothpick. The tail shown on the same page is suitable for furry animals such as cats and squirrels and should be attached to an elastic waist belt (see also page 38).

Some ideas for very easy costumes are shown opposite. The slug and the scarecrow can be put together from garments already in the family wardrobe or borrowed from friends or classmates. The two bird costumes are of the simplest cut and construction. They would be really lovely in felt or painted canvas, but if economy is important it would be possible to use up something which can be spared from home, with paint and cut paper for decoration.

With costumes for children's plays, inspiration is far more important than finish, and it is important that the joy and delight of creating and wearing them should not be diminished by heavy-handed accuracy.

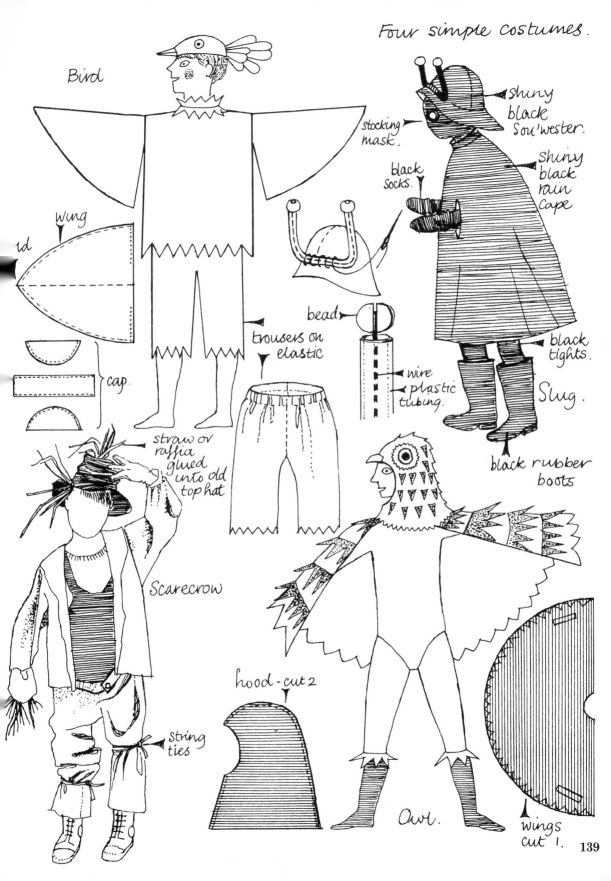

Four simple costumes.

Bird

wing

~~rd~~ wing

cap.

stocking mask.

black socks.

bead

wire
plastic tubing.

trousers on elastic

shiny black Sou'wester.

shiny black rain cape

black tights.

Slug.

black rubber boots

straw or raffia glued into old top hat

Scarecrow

string ties

hood - cut 2

Owl.

wings cut 1.

139

21 · Curtain up

After the mounting excitement of the dress parade and dress rehearsals, last-minute alterations and additional bright ideas, it is sometimes difficult to make a cool, calm check to see that everything is in readiness for the first night. This is nevertheless essential. In the excitement one or other of the performers is bound to have mislaid a glove or fan; in a room where several dancers are dressing together, shoes get wrongly paired up. This is why clear naming of *every* article is important. Check off lists of final alterations and of last-minute things to be bought so that there will be no panics after the shops have closed. See that there is a good supply of safety pins, elastic and tape for emergencies and that scissors and needles (already threaded) are handy for immediate use.

After the first night thrills, the production has to settle down into a smooth-running routine, with no falling off of freshness and liveliness, and constant maintenance of the costumes will help to preserve this. A responsible wardrobe mistress or master with helpers must be at the theatre or hall well before the performance to make sure that the clothes are in good condition. It is a good idea to plan two bands of helpers: one group to come in during the day to wash or take to the launderette shirts, tights etc. and to press costumes and clean shoes when necessary; the second group to arrive about an hour and a half before the performance to take the costumes to the right rooms and to check that all the right pieces are there – in a big show this can take quite a long time. At the end of each performance the person in charge should leave a list of running repairs for next day. If this part of the work is carried out well, the last performance should look every bit as fresh and spectacular as the first.

When all is over, sort out the costumes and accessories which are to be kept for stock, arrange for them to be washed or cleaned and then labelled and stored in a dry place. Plastic bags will help to keep them dust-free. Unpick any useful trimmings such as braids, feathers and flowers from costumes which are to be thrown out and keep them in marked boxes for future use.

Finally, think carefully over all that has happened during the production and decide where improvements could have been made so that however satisfactory the show has been, the next one will be even better!

Bibliography

Barton, Lucy *Historic Costume for the Stage*. Black, London and Baker, Boston 1961

Bott, Alan *Our Fathers (1870-1900)*. Heinemann, London and Arno, New York 1975

Bott, Alan and Clephane, Iris *Our Mothers*. Gollancz, London and Arno, New York 1975

Boucher, Francois *20,000 Years of Fashion*. Abrams, New York 1966

Contini, Mila *Fashion from Ancient Egypt to the Present Day*. Cresent, New York 1966

Cunnington, C.Willett and Phillis *Handbooks of English Costume* (several vols covering different periods). Faber, London and Plays, Boston

Cunnington, Phillis and Lucas, Catherine *Occupational Costume in England*. Black, London and Barnes & Noble, New York 1967

Davenport, Millia *The Book of Costume*. Crown, New York 1964

Hartley, Dorothy and Elliot, Margaret *Life and Work of the People of England*. (6 vols) Batsford, London c.1928

Howell, Georgina *In Vogue: Six Decades of Fashion*. Allen Lane, London and Schocken, New York 1976

Kohler, Carl and Von Sichart, Emma (ed. Alexander K. Dallas) *A History of Costume*. Dover, New York and London

Laver, James *A Concise History of Costume*. Thames & Hudson, London 1969

Laver, James *A Concise History of Costume and Fashion*. Scribner, New York 1974

Laver, James *Costume Illustration: The Seventeenth and Eighteenth Centuries. Costume Illustration: The Nineteenth Century*. H.M. Stationery Office, London

Payne, Blanche *History of Costume from the Ancient Egyptians to the Twentieth Century*. Harper & Row, New York and London 1965

Priestley, J.B. *The Edwardians*. Sphere Books, London 1972 and Harper & Row, New York 1970

Ruppert, *Le Costume I-V*. Flammarion, Paris.

Schoeffler, O.E. and Gale, William *Esquire's Encyclopedia of Twentieth Century Men's Fashions*. McGraw-Hill, New York 1973

Schönewolf, Herta *Play with Light and Shadow*. Studio Vista, London and Reinhold, New York 1969

Schroeder, Joseph J. (Jr) (ed.) *The Wonderful World of Ladies Fashion 1850-1920*. Digest Books, Northfield, Illinois 1971

Taylor, Boswell (ed.) *Picture Reference Books* nos 1, 2, 4, 5, 10 (particularly 4, *Costume*). Brockhampton Press, Leicester England

Tilke, M. *Costumes Patterns and Designs*. Zwemmer, London 1956 and Hastings, New York 1974

Waugh, Norah *The Cut of Men's Clothes, 1600-1900*. Faber, London and Theatre Arts, New York 1964

Waugh, Norah *The Cut of Women's Clothes, 1600-1930*. Faber, London and Theatre Arts, New York 1968

Wilcox, R. Turner *The Dictionary of Costume*. Scribner, New York 1969 and Batsford, London 1971

Wilcox, R. Turner *Five Centuries of American Costume*. Scribner, New York 1963, 1976 and Black, London 1966

Winter, Gordon *A Country Camera 1844-1914*. David & Charles, Newton Abbot 1971; Penguin, London 1973 and Gale, Detroit 1971; Penguin, New York 1974

Any volumes of *Punch*, *Harper's* and *Vogue*

Index